Othello's Secret

Shakespeare Now!
Series edited by Ewan Fernie and Simon Palfrey

First Wave:
At the Bottom of Shakespeare's Ocean Steve Mentz
Godless Shakespeare Eric S. Mallin
Shakespeare's Double Helix Henry S. Turner
Shakespeare Inside Amy Scott-Douglass
Shakespearean Metaphysics Michael Witmore
Shakespeare's Modern Collaborators Lukas Erne
Shakespeare Thinking Philip Davis
To Be Or Not To Be Douglas Bruster

Second Wave:
The King and I Philippa Kelly
The Life in the Sonnets David Fuller
Hamlet's Dreams David Schalkwyk
Nine Lives of William Shakespeare Graham Holderness
Shakespeare and I edited by Theodora Papadopoulou and William McKenzie
Shakespeare's Universality Kiernan Ryan
Teaching Shakespeare and Marlowe: Learning vs the System Liam Semler
Tragic Cognition in Shakespeare's Othello Paul Cefalu

Visit the *Shakespeare Now!* Blog at:
http://shakespearenowseries.blogspot.com/ for further news and updates on the series.

Othello's Secret

The Cyprus Problem

R M CHRISTOFIDES

Bloomsbury Arden Shakespeare
An imprint of Bloomsbury Publishing Plc

BLOOMSBURY
LONDON • OXFORD • NEW YORK • NEW DELHI • SYDNEY

Bloomsbury Arden Shakespeare

An imprint of Bloomsbury Publishing Plc

Imprint previously known as Arden Shakespeare

50 Bedford Square, London, WC1B 3DP, UK
1385 Broadway, New York, NY 10018, USA
29 Earlsfort Terrace, Dublin 2, Ireland

www.bloomsbury.com

BLOOMSBURY, THE ARDEN SHAKESPEARE and the Diana logo are trademarks of Bloomsbury Publishing Plc

First published 2016

© R M Christofides, 2016

R M Christofides has asserted his right under the Copyright, Designs and Patents Act, 1988, to be identified as author of this work.

All rights reserved. No part of this publication may be reproduced or transmitted in any form or by any means, electronic or mechanical, including photocopying, recording, or any information storage or retrieval system, without prior permission in writing from the publishers.

No responsibility for loss caused to any individual or organization acting on or refraining from action as a result of the material in this publication can be accepted by Bloomsbury or the author.

British Library Cataloguing-in-Publication Data
A catalogue record for this book is available from the British Library.

ISBN:	PB:	978-1-4742-1297-7
	ePDF:	978-1-4742-1299-1
	ePub:	978-1-4742-1298-4

Library of Congress Cataloging-in-Publication Data
Names: Christofides, R. M.
Title: Othello's secret : the Cyprus problem / R M Christofides.
Description: New York : Bloomsbury Arden Shakespeare, 2016. |
Series: Shakespeare now! | Includes bibliographical references and index.
Identifiers: LCCN 2015034306 | ISBN 9781474212977 (paperback)
Subjects: LCSH: Shakespeare, William, 1564-1616. Othello. | Cyprus—In literature. | BISAC: LITERARY CRITICISM / Shakespeare. | DRAMA / Shakespeare.
Classification: LCC PR2829 .C47 2016 | DDC 822.3/3—dc23 LC record available at http://lccn.loc.gov/2015034306

Series: Shakespeare Now!

Typeset by RefineCatch Limited, Bungay, Suffolk

For Jodie, Belinda and Xanthe. May our little family always be this happy.

CONTENTS

Acknowledgements viii

Prologue   1
Act One   17
Act Two   31
Act Three: Part One   43
Act Three: Part Two   59
Act Four   73
Act Five   85

Notes   103
Bibliography   111
Index   117

ACKNOWLEDGEMENTS

Thanks to Ewan Fernie and Simon Palfrey for their feedback and encouragement in the process of developing this from concept to viable project. Thanks to Emily Hockley for dealing expertly with all my queries. Thanks to all the friends and relatives who, over the years, have taken the time to discuss their experiences in Cyprus. Thanks to Charlie and Zena Matthews for their support and encouragement. Thanks to my mother and father, who lived what I can only write about; in many ways, this book is a love letter to you. Speaking of love letters, thanks to Jodie Matthews for everything; once more, this book is as much yours as mine.

Prologue

Like so many love affairs, my relationship with *Othello* began in a bar.

> You really don't know what happened?
> No.
> You never spoke about it?
> No.
> Not once?
> Do I need to say it again?
> Well.
> Well?
> I think it started with running guns and leafleting.
> Right.
> I'm not sure how things worked then – you'll have to ask – but it was something like that. Guns, propaganda, then hand grenades thrown at British soldiers.
> Well.
> Well.

I could not know it at the time but, in the haze of this inebriated exchange, my approach to *Othello*, as well as my critical methodology in general, was being formed as surely as it was in the undergraduate studies I was about to complete. In the months and years to come, this moment would become crucial in the development of my relationship with literature and the critical approaches it elicits. External or historical forces like this, like the family history on the verge of drunken revelation, play a significant role in the construction of a reader's identity but are never exactly replicated from one individual to the next. As the doyen of deconstruction, Jacques Derrida, puts it, every repetition differs from what it repeats because no two contexts are the same, each repetition breaking 'with every given context, engendering an infinity of new contexts' (1988: 12). So the psychosocial processes of identity formation have, for each of us, their own context, their own vocabulary, their own matrices. *Othello* facilitated the embryonic negotiation between who I was and what I would later say about literature. Yet this encounter in a bar was not the first step in forming my critical approach to literature: the battle for my future identity as a critic was underway long ago, in the violent side streets and torture cells of colonial Cyprus.

> The first arrest, he was young. Seventeen, eighteen.
> That young?
> That young. What were you doing when you were seventeen?
>   What was *I* doing? My father says he had the body of a middleweight when he came out of the prison camp. They all did. All of them chiselled out of stone.
> Made of stone. Like the song.
> Like the song.
> That's what I was doing when I was seventeen.
> Anyway, he was never charged. They took him to the Central Prisons in Nicosia, then Kyrenia Castle – was it that way round? – then to Camp 'K'.
> 'K' for Kafka?
> At least Kafka gets to the trial. Kokkinotrimithia.
> They shortened it.
> He spent the best part of two years in there. Detention without charge.
> Well.
> Well.

On the city streets outside, the spring rainfall was heavy enough to make pedestrians leap over roadside rivulets rushing down the slope of the street. Looking out at them huddled under umbrellas and hurdling over the running water, I remembered times my father did speak to me about the life he lived before he came to Britain. On one occasion he recalled with rare nostalgia the diminished little torrents that still raced through his village in late spring, a time of year when the low, flat Mesaoria plain, which sits at the centre of Cyprus between the island's two mountain ranges, finally loses its sparse greenery as the scorching face of the encroaching summer sun gets ever hotter. This time of year is also early watermelon season, and he described the childish bickering between his brothers as they all straddled the baby streams that still held out against the heat. All the young boys, dusty and barefoot, eating watermelon in thick, rounded triangles, then spitting the seeds into the water, watching as the little black ovals set off on the long journey down the mountain's evergreen incline towards the barren valley below. All the young boys, so long ago, a vision of Cyprus idealized by temporal and spatial distance from those innocent events then subsequently poeticized by the retelling. This poeticization was only increased by my appropriation of an inherited memory, a memory passed on to me in the hope that I would think fondly of the life my father lived before he was an immigrant and might share some part, however small, of the love he had for a past lost in time and a place left behind. A very different inheritance was being passed on in the bar.

It wasn't just the once, either.
No?
No.
There were other imprisonments, shorter, more intense. Solitary confinement, that sort of thing.
What sort of thing? What do you mean?
He's never mentioned it?
Are we going to do this again?
You – *finger moving in a circle over the empty glasses on the table* – you want?

> Don't know if I can. In a minute maybe.
> Strange that it's never come up even.
> When would it come up?
> He really never mentioned it? Strange.
> You want to finish what you've started?
> It was not uncommon or it happened a fair bit anyway, there were tortures and the like, beatings and worse. No one could visit him at, I think, Omorphita. No one knew why. They guessed why when he came out because he had the same underwear on as when he was arrested weeks before. It was white when he went in and nothing but red when he came out.

Certain things about my father began to fall into place. The brooding taciturnity when English girls called round. The steadfast refusal to ever, no matter the circumstance, support the English in sport. These were no longer irritable eccentricities or unreasonable defiance to the process of cultural assimilation. Instead, they now seemed like small, negative remainders equalized by the magnanimity he had shown in acquiescing to my mother's desire for a life in Britain; a place where work was available to them and a state education valorized in the Commonwealth was accessible to their children. He would never have passed Norman Tebbit's test of national sporting allegiance, but any straightforward measure of integration or loyalty to Britain became frivolous when applied to a man locked up and brutalized by soldiers of that state in his formative years. Any patriotic identification with the nebulous notion of Britishness requires reciprocal recognition of the long-standing effects colonialism and its afterlife has had on individuals, their families and the cultural memory of their communities. As for my father, he did not demand any such form of recognition: brooding taciturnity and steadfast refusal were his default setting. There was no other way to be in the cell.

If there can be a moment that defines who we are as critics, a moment or event that, when push comes to shove, we identify as the *sine qua non* for the commitments we put down on the page, the revelation of my father's experiences in colonial Cyprus was mine. From then on, Shakespeare's *Othello* could no longer be a play in which Cyprus was a backdrop and little else. From then on, *Othello* could no longer be a play in which, as many recent approaches assume, the location merely indicates wider British and European anxieties regarding Ottoman expansion or the proto-capitalist, proto-colonial mercantile exchanges throughout the Mediterranean in the sixteenth and seventeenth centuries. From then on, the synergies between the Cyprus Wars of the sixteenth century and the modern wars that culminated in the island's division were vital. The play for me now had to be articulated in relation to the troubled twentieth- and twenty-first-century existence of Cyprus. And in Othello himself, I saw some part of my father.

His detainment and torture at the hands of British officers in the 1950s was down to his role in EOKA (*Εθνική Οργάνωσις Κυπρίων Αγωνιστών* – the National Organization of Cypriot Fighters), a nationalist paramilitary group with two aims. The first was independence from British rule. In line with its fanatically Hellenistic and anti-Turkish sentiment, the second aim was the greater ideal of union with Greece, a political ideology commonly known as *enosis*. Both Othello and my father thus had a similar military charge, one firmly fastened to how they understood their personal place in the world: their task was to retain Cyprus and themselves as European strongholds of Christianity by resisting the advancement of the Muslim Turk. And both Othello and my father would eventually be implicated with the 'enemy' Turk in unanticipated or intolerable ways. Their intertwined personal and political resistance to the Turk without and the Turk within also shared an historical root: the bedrock for the anti-Turkish sentiment that fuelled EOKA's drive for *enosis* was the sixteenth-century Ottomanization of Cyprus, events Shakespeare added to *Othello* and events that first introduced a Turkish-speaking community to the island. Soon, my father and I began to discuss the Cyprus Problem and, before long, I saw Othello's words do the same, echoing back at me those interwoven personal and political questions with which my father had always grappled. Not only did Othello's turmoil represent Cypriot turmoil, but in the awkward, anxious duality of his position as insider and outsider, I saw the internal world of many immigrants, first and second generation, parent and child, all of us who must, in every word or action, balance the often contradictory cultural demands made by two or more homes, all the while striking a tone that satisfies separate cultural spheres often at odds with each other. That the critical field has failed to exploit *Othello* as a literary resource for talking about the Cyprus Problem left me in no doubt that the British-based world of Shakespeare studies – despite the claims from those 'isms' within the field to speak from, or on behalf of, marginal positions – inadvertently reproduces the British colonial attitude to Cyprus. In the words of one leading historian, the island was the British Empire's 'inconsequential possession' (Varnava 2009) and Shakespeare studies have repeatedly, consistently and without exception treated the connection between *Othello* and the Cyprus Problem as similarly inconsequential. One problem is about to be solved, at least.

*

Some time after that conversation in a bar, a cousin asked me to appear in a sketch on his radio show as a bar owner from Cyprus encouraging Brits to visit the island for their summer holidays. It was barely light when the phone rang. 'So what's your bar called?' someone asked. The answer was immediate. 'It's called Othello's Bar, of course!' This reply, delivered in the thickest Cypriot accent I can perform (which is basically my father's voice), seemed obvious to me as well as the others on the show. It was a response that tapped into the long-standing literary connection between Shakespeare and what, in line with popular convention, was referred to in the sketch as 'Aphrodite's island'. If you have ever been to Cyprus, then, quite probably, you will have seen or even sat in a bar or café or restaurant called Othello's, whether at the clubber's paradise of Ayia Napa, the family resort of Paphos, the beautifully decayed side streets of old Nicosia or the citadel at Famagusta, commonly referred to as Othello's Tower. In the Cypriot psyche, the connection between the play and the island is deep-rooted, not least because four of the five acts are set there. But this connection has deeper resonance than just the play's setting. Othello – like so many of the figures in early modern literature inspired by the Greater Middle East – can be difficult to pin down in terms of racial, religious and geographical provenance, a plethora of differences scholarly critics have fetishized and categorized. This dual movement of both exploring and controlling Othello's hybridity, a gesture that occurs in the narrative of the play as well as the critical discourses it has inspired, has, up until now, been entirely associated with sixteenth-century Venice, with more recent approaches seeing in Shakespeare's depiction of the *Serenissima* concerns that map onto our own. Cyprus, inexplicably, has rarely been part of the equation. Yet Shakespeare's Moor stands as English literature's most urgent representation of the treatment of cultural diversity in Cyprus, a diversity repeatedly disavowed and repressed throughout the modern hostilities that tore the island apart.

Take Othello's final action, a suicide of shame prompted by the wrongful murder of his innocent wife, Desdemona. It can be seen as a profound statement on cultural diversity in Cyprus. The tragic hero of the play, the mighty Othello, cut down by Iago's proto-racist sniping and linguistic trickery, reduced to the perpetrator of theatre's most famous and abominable crime of passion, kills himself after telling a short tale. Ready to plunge a knife into his stomach, he asks those present to remember that he, a black man in the service of the Venetian Empire, has killed honourably as well as dishonourably, providing by way of example the killing of an ill-meaning Turk in Aleppo. This suicide story by itself testifies to the region's heterogeneity based on migration, trade and military expansion. But with Othello playing the double role of killer and victim, the suicide story also situates the disgraced general as both Turk and anti-Turk, victim and perpetrator, insider and outsider, simultaneously on both sides of the Cyprus Wars fought by the Venetians and Ottomans. It is precisely this ambiguity of position, this nationalism from beyond the margins of the nation, which Iago exploits by incessantly reminding Othello that, although he serves and defends the Venetian state, he can never truly know it or be a part of it due to his otherness. When he drives the knife through his flesh, Othello attempts to expel or cleanse that otherness. One of the leading authorities on *Othello*, Virginia Mason Vaughan, suggests that in Othello's demise early modern audiences would have seen the fall of Cyprus to the Ottoman Turk in the 1570s (2011: 28–9). If so, then in Othello's demise the rise of the island's modern enmities can also be seen. The two are concomitant: the suicidal ethnic cleansing introduces a new framework of conflict, a supranational nationalism, that culminated in the Turk and anti-Turk ethnic cleansing of 1974 still enforced by today's bi-communal partition.

In a clear deviation from the novella in Cinthio's *Hecatommithi* that was the play's primary source, Othello is killed off in Cyprus as he grapples with inner and outer Turks. This takes place on a contested site Shakespeare knew had uncomfortably transitioned from European to Ottoman control. Whether Shakespeare meant it or not, in the Moorish general he designed an unarguably Cypriot persona because his inner turmoil allegorizes the current division of the island. Clearly, the play interrogates Venetian, and therefore European, fears of a snarling, turbaned invader, but Othello internalizes Turco-European discord at a time when the same process was occurring in Cyprus. From Limassol to Güzelyurt, Girne to Larnaca, this self-dividing schizophrenia has held sway ever since. Ask a Greek Cypriot where Othello's Tower is and they'll tell you Famagusta. Ask a Turkish Cypriot and they'll tell you Gazimağusa.[1]

Like Othello, Cyprus too can be seen as the victim of its otherness: it remains an island caught between definitions of

East and West, Orient and Occident, Islam and Christianity. Neither wholly inside nor wholly outside Europe, its unmistakeably Middle Eastern vibe is filtered through a Hellenism rooted predominantly in Byzantine Orthodoxy, an Anglophilia picked up during its eighty-two years' governance by the British Empire and the post-Ottoman tenets of Atatürk's modern Turkey. This cultural bricolage should be something to celebrate. The wider historical antagonisms of Turkey and Greece are the most obvious case of how diversity has instead been perceived as a threat to the nationalist and expansionist aims of larger nations and their sympathizers in Cyprus who, together, have fought to define the island as either Turkish or Greek.

Like Israel/Palestine or the domino-roll of upheaval, sometimes liberating and other times horrific, seen by the so-called Arab Spring, the Cyprus Problem bolts the door against difference. These complex hotspots are, to borrow the Italian phrase for 'door bolt', *catenaccio* points – points where the rich polyculturalism of the *zona mista*, or mixed zone, that is the Greater Middle East comes face-to-face with efforts to chain down inherent differences, to demarcate and homogenize communities and even nation-states.[2] The notion of the Greater Middle East as a *zona mista* would have been an obvious one to a dramatist shaped by a world in which the concept of the nation-state was in constant flux, not the fixed, rigorously defined entity we understand. It was, furthermore, a world in which the dramatic shifts of the Reformation were followed hard upon by the apparent threat of even greater change embodied by ongoing Ottoman expansion. In this crossover between literary conceptions of the Greater Middle East in Shakespeare's time and their potential to powerfully counterpoint violent attempts to categorize the region today, a geopolitical criticism can be located.

*

The feverish drive to homogenize Cyprus reached its nadir in the summer of 1974 when inter-communal conflict, a *coup d'état* sponsored by the military junta in Greece, and a subsequent Turkish invasion and division of the island separated the two communities. Britain, the ex-colonial power and signed-up guarantor of Cypriot sovereignty alongside Greece and Turkey, stood by as the events inflicted on both sides not only the death and sorrow of war, but the horrors of ethnic cleansing, mass rape and the still unknown fate of missing persons. With the fall of the Berlin Wall in 1989, Nicosia became the world's only remaining divided capital city. As with all Middle Eastern conflicts, there are many complicated, even paradoxical, reasons for the events that led to the war of 1974 and the repeatedly failed attempts at reunification, but one constant has remained: during both British rule and post-colonial independence, the struggle to disambiguate Cyprus, to define it in Greek or Turkish terms, has been more powerful than other, more inclusive, 'pro-Cypriot' visions. Consequently, successive rounds of reunification talks, or even talks *about* reunification talks, continued to be haunted by rigid, inflexible understandings of how Cyprus should be defined.

This tendency to view the island's two largest ethnic groups as strictly incompatible, or even to view them as distinct ethnic groups at all, is a modern convention. Ethnonationalism – nationalism tied not to the country you live in but to the ethnicity with which you identify – has its political foundations in the tensions of the colonial period and a longing to be part of the emergent nations of Greece and Turkey that have done so much to shape the cultural milieu of modern Cyprus. Standard historical accounts posit Greek Cypriots as descendants of Bronze Age Mycenaean settlers, and this Greek-speaking community was the most populous in sixteenth-century Cyprus. Famagusta was the most famous Cypriot city of the time, the probable setting of *Othello* as well as the explicit setting of John Ford's 1628 tragicomedy *The Lover's Melancholy*. According to William Malim's 1572 translation of Conte Nestore Martinengo's *The true report of all the successe of Famagosta*, it was these peasant 'Grecians', rather than the Frankish elite, who were employed to aid the Venetian defence against Ottoman raids on the affluent port. These raids would eventually lead to the establishment of a rival Turkish-speaking community. After the nineteenth-century Greek War of Independence, another Euro-Ottoman battle with the formative Greek state at its centre rather than Venice, the Greek-speaking community had a powerful external nation with which to identify. When Atatürk's Turkish Republic emerged a century later in the place of the dwindling Ottoman Empire, the Turkish-speaking community had its own external nation to mythologize as a motherland. These positions hardened irretrievably during British rule. Significantly, the ethnonationalistic view of a Cyprus annexed to Turkey or Greece differs wildly from the vision of it we find in *Othello*. The play is set before the Ottoman conquest of Cyprus, but those events and the Greco-Turkish friction they prefigured sit ominously at the edge of the action. In *Othello*, the terms 'Greek', 'Turkish' and 'Cypriot' are still very much up for grabs.

Needless to say, *Othello* does not depict everyone living happily in a colourful bouncy castle of love, but it does present us with a multifaceted vision of the Mediterranean. Sites of flux and exchange, personalities difficult to define and a heady gallimaufry of mythical or religious tropes all undercut any notion of stable ethnic or religious identity. So when, for instance, Othello asks his drunk, fighting soldiers if they have 'turned Turks' (2.3.162), he connects the strange and powerful infidel empire threatening to overtake Europe with unruly, uncivilized behaviour.[3] But a plethora of often antithetical values are massed under the equivocal banner of 'Turk', a slippery term that referred specifically to the Ottoman and also more generally to Muslims. An angry Othello immediately follows up his criticism by scolding the clumsy rabble for squabbles 'heaven hath forbid the Ottomites' (2.3.163), renowned as Ottoman soldiers were for their brotherhood and team spirit. At one and the same time, barbarity to be abhorred and civility to be reproduced are associated with an empire known for its geographical scope and internal diversity, pre-empting Othello's self-identification as Turk and Turk-slayer. All the while, Iago is the one who has 'turned Turk' according to Othello's yardstick of Turkish barbarity and civility by breeding aggression and hatred within the Venetian force. Venice becomes home, and Cyprus host, to the inhumanity projected on to the absent figure of the Turk.

Who is this Turk, then? Is it Othello all along, who tells us that, in line with the Ottoman practice of converting captured slaves, he was 'taken by the insolent foe | And sold to slavery' (1.3.138–9)? Is it Iago, who performs the role of evil sprite in the absence of any Turkish bogeyman and with such thrilling ingenuity that we obsess over his malignity in much the same way Jacobean audiences would have obsessed over the Ottoman threat? His tongue-in-cheek claim that women are sexually duplicitous or else he is 'a Turk' (2.1.114) invites the audience, who know his pernicious game, to cast him in that role. And does Iago – whose name, as has often been pointed out, evokes St James the Moor slayer – evoke the Cypriot King James II described by Richard Knolles in *The generall historie of the Turkes*, one of Shakespeare's sources? Known as the Bastard, this dastardly King of Cyprus married a fourteen-year-old Venetian, Catherine Cornaro. Did Shakespeare have this Bastard in mind when scripting Othello's marriage to the teenage Desdemona too? These are questions and possibilities provoked by the setting, a setting torn between East and West in the sixteenth century and then again in the twentieth and twenty-first centuries, an island on which the simplistic binary of Turk and anti-Turk has, since those Cyprus Wars of the 1570s, been gradually instituted as a stubborn pillar of extremist nationalism.

That *Othello* has yet to be rigorously studied in relation to the development of these fraught divisions is indicative of the mainstream academic conservatism still primarily interested in Venice. Francis Gentleman's eighteenth-century commentary on the play sees no reason for the change of location in the second act, setting the tone for this abiding collective oversight: 'What follows concerning Cyprus, we can by no means see any necessity for; as every part of the plot might have been preserved with equal force, by keeping the characters all through at Venice' (1770: 134). Writing two centuries after the Cyprus Wars and a century before Cyprus passed from Ottoman to British hands, Gentleman can be excused more readily for his confusion than the contemporary critical field. *Visions of Venice in Shakespeare* (Tosi and Bassi 2011) claims to see both *Othello* and *The Merchant of Venice* in a variety of ways that have traction in today's world. But in the case of *Othello*, this otherwise excellent collection of essays reproduces the usual Venice-mania that either excludes Cyprus or views it as a footnote to Turco-European tensions of the period. Stanley Wells's foreword to *Visions of Venice in Shakespeare* (2011) repeatedly mentions the Venetian setting, a prime example of the mass scholarly blindness that will not or cannot see a productive engagement between the Cypriot setting and the continuing fight to control that setting. The unquestioned, unproblematized inclusion of *Othello* as a Venetian play alongside *The Merchant of Venice* betrays this consistent oversight.[4] If the exploration of the colonial periphery has become something of a methodological cliché, then the extension of this courtesy to Othello's Cyprus is long overdue.

Another recent collection, Arden's *Othello: The State of Play* (2014), exemplifies the exclusion of Cyprus even when investigations of the colonial periphery occur. Ambereen Dadabhoy skilfully links Ottoman cultural practices in the play to the familiar 'crisis in colonial subjectivity' Othello has often been said to suffer (2014: 124), positioning him as an escaped janissary captured as a child and converted to Islam for military purposes. No discussion of Cyprus ensues, but practices such as this *devşirme* were firmly established there by the time of the play's first performance. Knolles's description of the siege of Nicosia even describes the 'yong babes [. . .] violently taken out of the armes of their mothers' (1603: 852), while Cornelis de Bruyn documented forced conversion in Famagusta a century or so after the siege (Walsh 2012: 463–6).

Othello's 'colonial subjectivity' may have been Cypriot all along.

Even when Cyprus does enter the fray, it often takes a pejorative or purely historical form. Murray J. Levith sees both Othello and the island he inhabits as models of the same 'primitive and elemental chaos' (1989: 32). Levith, in his own way, at least acknowledges that what Othello signifies and what Cyprus signifies go hand-in-hand. Emrys Jones did give the 'violent conversion from Christian to Turkish rule' that resulted from the Cyprus Wars the critical attention it deserved in the 1960s but saw these events as 'very remote from what a modern audience bring to *Othello*', leaving the twentieth-century struggles on the island untouched (1968: 52, 51). This neglect was all the more perplexing given that Cyprus was front-page news for much of the late 1950s as colonial forces repeatedly clashed with EOKA, then again with the resurgence of inter-communal conflict in the 1960s that brought on frantic American-led diplomatic efforts to avert a war between Greece and Turkey. No doubt this omission says more about what the discipline of English Literature values as appropriate or proper to the field of study than it does about Jones's interests.

Othello heavyweights such as Michael Neill and Daniel J. Vitkus have also let Cyprus fall between the cracks. Neill called *Othello* a 'foundational text in the emergence of modern European racial consciousness' in which the titular Moor could be any one of a range of 'darker skinned people' (1998: 361, 364–5), while Vitkus laid out the play's complicity with, and interrogation of, fears of Islamic conversion or 'turning Turk' (1997). In both cases, the actual conversion of Cyprus to the literal and figurative blackness linked to Islam, a conversion Othello embodies, fails to register. Another big-hitter, Ania Loomba, saw the play as a manifestation of European demands for 'the conversion of the outsider to the service of dominant culture', as well as a literary document of how the emergent racial consciousness Neill examined was 'animated by notions of sexual and gender difference' (Loomba 1989: 50; Loomba 2002: 93). These modes of exploitation and exoticization, the familiar push and pull of colonial desire, are embedded in the modern colonial story of Cyprus. This modern colonial story was already anticipated in Shakespeare's time by Turco-Venetian hostility and the Levant Company established to trade with Ottoman territories. No critic has an individual obligation to make Cyprus a central concern, but if, as Neill points out, *Othello* criticism has a tendency to reinscribe racialism in its frequently obsessive attention to the protagonist's skin colour (1989: 392–3), then it also has a clear tendency to occlude Cyprus.

A lone voice in the woods, Eleni Pilla's review of a Cypriot production of *Othello* describes the switching of seats in its early stages, an aggressive game of musical chairs which she reads as a visual encoding of 'the displacement of a huge number of people from the northern part of Cyprus as a result of the Turkish invasion of Cyprus in 1974' (2013: 366). Although this short but significant review addresses the Cyprus Problem in relation to *Othello*, it also reproduces the chauvinism of the conflict. The displacement only occurs one way, from north to south, whitewashing the displacement of Turkish Cypriots in the other direction. And the war is reduced to just 'the Turkish invasion' with the role of Greece and any culpability on the side of Greek Cypriots elided. Whether they are born there or part of the diaspora, almost everyone with a connection to Cyprus grows up in an environment in which the Cyprus Problem dominates conversation. Those, often very heated, conversations are conducted either from or against these heavily chauvinistic positions, and in the North London circles in which those debates took place around me, Cyprus was always exclusively, honourably, proudly Greek, and Turks always exclusively barbarous invaders. Indeed, there was no such thing as Cypriots, only the Greeks of Cyprus and the invading Turks who illegally occupied a space Hellenic by right. That I am writing this book, that I view *Othello* as a literary means of counteracting the zealotry that underpins Cypriot political discourse, owes much to the fact that these inelegant positions were severely challenged by life in Britain: removed from the intensely combustible and then completely divided realm of Cyprus, we lived, worked, studied and fell in love with precisely those we were taught to hate. In Britain, which holds the largest Cypriot diaspora community, interaction between Greek and Turkish Cypriots is commonplace, whereas entire generations in Cyprus have grown up post-1974 without ever knowing anyone from the demonized community living silently on the other side of no man's land.[5]

The times, though, are always changing. In 2013, the economic crisis in the Eurozone hit Cyprus and refocused attention on its expendability when set against the concerns of larger, more powerful nations. Two years later, reunification talks were again on the horizon. Whether any settlement would provide the conditions for genuine reintegration or, given that a bi-zonal state always forms the unconditional basis of negotiations, merely ratify the ethnonationalistic narrative of two irreconcilable adversaries, only time will tell. Either way, with talks mooted, the Turkish Cypriots elected an independent and pro-solution candidate, Mustafa Akıncı, as president. An olive branch, like that worn by Akıncı's supporters, was extended by one part of the island to the other. Once more, tentative hopes were raised for an end, finally, to the traumas of separation; it is a separation that, even when it promises reunion, constantly resurrects the competing claims on Cyprus in the sixteenth century that Shakespeare seems to have appreciated with greater nuance, and greater prescience, than has been previously assumed. Now more than ever, Othello's fall from grace screams loudly what has been peculiarly silent to so many: Othello's problem is and always has been the problem of Cyprus.

Act One

IAGO Awake, what ho, Brabantio! thieves, thieves, thieves!
Look to your house, your daughter and your bags!
Thieves, thieves!

(1.1.78–80)

Before Othello even arrives on stage, Cyprus has become a major concern. Iago's resentment at the choice of Cassio as lieutenant, a resentment he spits out to his pliant dupe, Roderigo, includes reference to Iago's valiant military service at Rhodes and Cyprus, immediately connecting Cyprus with the Hellenic world with which it has long been associated. Whether these claims are hyperbolic need not matter; it is the choice of Cyprus as location that does. No sooner has Iago vented his spleen, he adds that Othello has 'embarked | With such loud reason to the Cyprus wars' (1.1.147–8). From the very moment we are in Venice, the play directs us away from Venice and towards Cyprus, away from the city-state the play fails to describe in half the detail afforded it in *The Merchant of Venice* and towards the Cyprus Wars it has no obligation to invoke. The novella in Cinthio's *Hecatommithi* that is the primary source for the play makes no mention of the Cyprus Wars because it pre-dates the Turco-Venetian struggle for possession of the island. Why, then, does Shakespeare choose the Cyprus Wars as a backdrop? Was it a very simple ploy to give the story an up-to-date feel? Was it a canny nod to James

I's interest in the Battle of Lepanto that inspired the king's celebratory poem, *The Lepanto*, which prefaces the victory for the Holy League of Catholic forces over the Ottomans with the fall of Cyprus? Was it meant to exploit fears among the audience of Ottoman expansion that saw in that same fall the potential fall of larger, Western nations, giving the domestic events geopolitical significance? All of these? None of these? Was it, after all, a random inconsequence to a popular playwright primarily concerned with getting paying customers through the door or actually the studied choice made by an artist at his mature peak adding depth and lustre to his work? We may never know, and the exploration of those gaps, those unknowns and any as-yet-unknown unknowns are the lifeblood of Shakespeare criticism.

That choice, however it came about, nevertheless becomes apparent from the outset. Before we have acclimatized to Venice, we are already on a journey to Cyprus, and the early action immediately conflates the scandal of illicit desire, miscegenation and sexualized robbery with Cyprus and the Cyprus Wars, with 'Th' importancy of Cyprus to the Turk' (1.3.21), with battles past and battles to come. Othello's clandestine marriage to Desdemona – for which, in the vocabulary Iago the ventriloquist encourages him to use, Brabantio brands Othello a 'foul thief' (1.2.62) – and the threat to Cyprus are revealed in boisterous tandem so that contested lusts and contested possessions in the domestic sphere are as much about the struggle for supremacy in Cyprus as they are about Venetian social mores. This parallel would have seemed self-evident to the early modern theatregoer familiar with both the mythological history of Aphrodite's island and its eventual capture by the Ottoman Empire. Today, forbidden desire and its reification in the form of property are a recurrent theme in the continued stalemate of division and repeatedly failed reunification in modern Cyprus. Thieves, thieves, thieves, foul and fair, are everywhere in Cyprus.

Property has become a sticking point in Cyprus. One of the most famous legal instances of this was the landmark international case of *Apostolides v Orams*, in which Meletios Apostolides won a case against British citizens David and Linda Orams. The Orams had built a holiday villa in Lapithos, a village in northern Cyprus now under the control of the Turkish Republic of Northern Cyprus, the state established almost a decade after the war of 1974 and immediately recognized by Turkey yet still considered occupied territory by the international community. That the Orams were British and went on to be represented by Cherie Blair in the English courts added to the public sense of injustice, with President Tassos Papadopoulos, a former member of the paramilitary EOKA group that fought British rule, publicly critical of both the acquisition of the property and the involvement of the British prime minister's wife. The former colonial master was still stoking fires. Apostolides claimed that he and his family had been displaced by the events of 1974 and the European Court of Justice eventually found in his favour in 2009, with the Orams forced to abandon the property. This case is one among many such cases that demonstrate the importance of property and property rights to the post-1974 psyche, not least because they revive the entangled traumas of colonialism and war. Between the end of the colonial era in 1960 and the war of 1974, the doomed interregnum in which a unified Cyprus existed, the most important impasse (of many) was Article 173 of the new constitution that stipulated the creation of separate urban municipalities, a legacy of colonial legislation carried forward to the new republic. How residential areas should be delimited, who had the right to manage amenities, and whether municipalities should be separated according to ethnicity, struck at the heart of whether Greek Cypriots and Turkish Cypriots could live together peacefully. The contemporary concern with property and property rights can be traced back to these spiky constitutional hagglings, which led to Turkish air strikes, attacks on Turkish Cypriot enclaves and the partitioning of Nicosia in the early 1960s.[1]

Concessions on the issue of returning to property, including ceding property rights to those living on land or in homes once owned by Greek Cypriots, was a key factor in the comprehensive rejection by Greek Cypriots of the 2004 Annan Plan for reunification. For the most part, the right to return to property has been a Greek Cypriot concern, with any obstructions to this considered a contravention of international human rights. While these contraventions have been affirmed by the European Court of Human Rights,[2] the prevailing narrative in Greek Cypriot society has been one of invasion and partition carried out by Turkish forces deliberately left to their own devices by the British, with the Cyprus Problem a straightforward case of Turkish aggression and subsequent intransigence conveniently ignored for the sake of wider Anglo-American interests. Although the aggression and intransigence cannot be refuted, the debates in Greek Cypriot society have traditionally been dominated by Greek nationalist ideologies that see no difference between Cyprus and Greece to the extent that the external Turk and the internal Turkish Cypriot are seen as one overriding Turkish foe occupying 'our' land. And 'our' land means Hellenic land. These debates occur in a landscape where the shared psyche is formed by 'educational policies [. . .] that inculcate Greek national values and probably discourage the development of Cypriot consciousness' (Papapavlou 1998: 25). A landscape where to speak 'cleanly' or to speak in a political or professional context is to speak Athenian Demotic instead of the Greek Cypriot dialect considered vulgar and 'Eastern' rather than chic and European (see Papadakis 2005: 12–13; Christofides 2010). These prejudices are tied to the construction of Greek identity in Cyprus, explained on the island and in diaspora communities around the globe as an integral, foundational part of a Christian tradition in Europe.

This tradition cannot be separated from continued resistance to Turkey's European Union membership in continental Europe, a drive of de-Ottomization that dates back to early modern fears of an aggressive, violent and growing Ottoman Empire, with the Cyprus Wars and the fall of Cyprus functioning as one of the most celebrated warnings of Europe's potential turn to the East, away from the Hellenic tradition.

The Cyprus Problem replays, almost exactly, the complicated dynamics of aggression that call Othello to this battle. Little wonder that the *coup d'état* sponsored by the fascist military dictatorship in Greece that preceded the 20 July 1974 Turkish invasion by five days is often conveniently forgotten by common Greek Cypriot memory, as is the ethnic cleansing of Turkish Cypriots from land and property now occupied by Greek Cypriots in the south.[3] The illegal occupation of property equates, so the argument goes, to the illegal occupation of Cyprus by so-called barbarous Turks, a symbolic link that the collective mindset dates back to the Venetian loss of Cyprus to the Ottomans. Hugely divisive and an archetypal Rûm knave, EOKA fighter and politician, Polycarpos Georkadjis, responded to the crisis sparked by the municipalities issue with an aggressive speech given in 1962 that invoked the Ottoman victory of 1571, claiming Cyprus 'had been Greek since the dawn of History [...] And Greek it shall remain' (quoted in Drousiotis 2008: 25). 1571, as both of Nicosia's two National Struggle Museums show, is a foundational and contested year.

By the southern edge of the Venetian walls and a stone's throw from Famagusta Gate, the Greek Cypriot National Struggle Museum earmarks 1571 in its introductory narrative as the bloody arrival of a problematic Turkish presence that continually obstructs the *enosis* Georkadjis zealously advocated. It takes half an hour or so to make the monumental historical walk from here to the northern edge of the Venetian walls where the competing museum sits. Going from the Taktakalas region of the old town once associated with deep inter-communal enmity – not least in the form of its sporting institution, Olympiakos Nicosia, for which my father played soccer and which still has written into its constitution the provision to change kit colours from green and black to Hellenic blue when *enosis* is achieved – you pass the Pancyprian Gymnasium, where Lawrence Durrell taught before taking up a post as press officer for the colonial office, and eventually arrive at the top of Ledra Street. Ledra Street traverses the dead zone, the barren no man's land of the Green Line that houses

Ledra Palace, formerly the island's leading hotel and now the standard site of negotiations for reunification. Once through the passport-controlled checkpoint at the bottom of Ledra Street – or Murder Mile, as it was known due to the frequent EOKA attacks on British soldiers and citizens – a northwards walk takes you past the majestic Büyük Khan, the island's largest Ottoman caravanserai, past the Venetian Column toppled by the Ottomans and re-erected by the British during the Great War, and past the British Colonial Law Courts until, finally, you reach Kyrenia (or Girne) Gate where the Turkish Cypriot National Struggle museum sits. This has a large grey plaque by the entrance that sets the tone, hailing 1571, alongside the war of 1974 and the establishment of the pseudo-state in 1983, as the first step towards a Turkish Cyprus free from what it refers to as 'Rûm' persecution, with 'Rûm' a generic term for the Middle Eastern and Byzantine Greek-speakers once governed by the Ottoman Empire. With its etymological roots in the Greek word for 'Roman', the term 'Rûm' links Greek Cypriots with the Roman lineage of the Greek-speaking Byzantine Empire, pushing Greek Cypriot history westwards and away from a Cyprus considered part of Turkey's sphere of influence since the fall of Constantinople to the Ottomans in 1453. This signification offers a concise mirror image of the Greek Cypriot construction of Turkish Cypriots as Eastern and Cyprus as culturally, if not geographically, Western.[4]

Less concerned with historical context, The Museum of Barbarism in the Kumsal district of north Nicosia turns the fear of home invasion in Cyprus into an artefact with the most gruesome depiction of the island's tit-for-tat persecutions; it is a small house preserved as a monument since 1963 when a woman and her three children were slaughtered. The victims' blood still blackens the bathroom. In adjacent rooms, graphic images of Turkish Cypriots murdered in the 1950s and 1960s require a strong constitution and, with the bloody bathroom, raise ethical questions about this kind of museological representation. The Museum of Barbarism inadvertently shows how far into the concept of a 'home' the antagonisms of 1571 have reached; the dispossessed home has come to represent the dispossessed nation, and the question of property has become synonymous with the question of national destiny. What museology, constitutional crises or the legal cases concerning property rights cannot reveal, however, are the ways in which property – in particular its relation to the paternal state and family – corresponds to the forbidden desire between Greek Cypriots and Turkish Cypriots. Just as Brabantio felt robbed by Othello, so any Cypriot family ceding a son or daughter to the barbarous other is also apparently robbed and must, so the ethnonationalist discourse goes, replay Brabantio's ire by banishing from the home the offending child whose grotesque and excessive desires contravene the father's prohibition.

*

Just that day I was at the Cyprus High Commission in one of central London's über-exclusive Georgian enclaves, a white-sepulchred Conradian home of Empire, to obtain an exit visa. From the age of fifteen onwards, any male of Cypriot descent requires government permission to leave Cyprus. Those of Cypriot descent residing in the republic who are physically able or who have less than four dependents are obliged to do military service, so the exit visa was proof of my British residency. The official helping me fill in my forms knew my father and made small talk, smiling.

> Your brothers, are they well?
> Yes, uncle.
> They're very good boys. The eldest one I know is married. To an English girl. But what about the other one?
> Yes, he's married now too.
> And you? Do you have a girlfriend yet?
> No, uncle.
> Good. You concentrate on your studies. Okay, just fill your name in in here. Can you write it in Greek?
> Yes, uncle.
> So the other one is married too. Good. To one of our own?

A pause. Yes, uncle.
Good. We need to stick together.
Yes.

It was an equivocation. My brother *was* married to a Cypriot, but that was not the question. The question referred only to Greeks. What the official meant when he asked 'To one of our own?' was 'To a Greek?' In this scenario, a mainland Greek girl or a Greek Cypriot girl were equally acceptable. A Turkish Cypriot – no different to a barbarous *Turk* – was not. By agreeing that she was indeed 'one of our own', I did not rule out the possibility that she was Turkish Cypriot, but let the official think the opposite. To this day, I still wonder if I said the right thing. Why didn't I just say, 'She's Turkish Cypriot. We're all very happy for them'? This would have been a lie at that moment in our family history, but it would have made a point. *L'esprit de l'escalier* the French call it, the spirit of the stairs, when you find the right words only after leaving the room.

That same night, my father rang before leaving work. Lay another place at the table, he told me. Straight away I knew what was about to happen. It was something revelatory, something I thought would never happen. I had spent a short lifetime answering the phone when she called, telling everyone that it was Mal or Jimmy or Ken. I had spent long days during the school holidays at a fenced-in soccer pitch kicking a ball back and forth along the concrete with her brother, challenging students from UCL to play us for the court, and all the while the young lovers stood aloof, spending time together in a place away from the scornful gaze of others, in a place where they could not be seen or judged or scolded. Sometimes our 'unofficial brother', a Moroccan immigrant my father found lying stabbed on the street one night, would stand with them, a friendly ambassador to their furtive affair. And when the intention to marry was announced in a letter from abroad, an entire community seemed to ask a familiar question of revilement: 'Ετουρτζέψαμεν;' The same question had been posed 400 years earlier: 'Are we turned Turks?' Peering through the curtains I saw my father's car eventually pull up and out of the passenger side stepped my sister-in-law, about to enter the house officially for the first time. What was about to be broken was the very clear correlation that existed in our household, as it did in so many Cypriot families, between any romantic entanglements with the enemy other and subsequent exclusion from the family home. That my father, so opposed to the marriage and so committed to the *meghali idea*, the grand idea of a greater Greece incorporating Cyprus, was about to break the correlation made the sight all the more startling. This was Leonidas bringing an Immortal to eat at the Spartan camp. The secret agreement to marry had led to the couple's official expulsion from both family homes, an expulsion already anticipated and internalized by their secret 'off-site' meetings.

Romantic possession of the child became an invasion and possession of the house, an unacceptable challenge to the tradition of dowry in appropriate marriages: the community ties established by the material exchange of dowry in an arranged marriage, where gift-giving supplants the choices made by female desire, collapse when an individual makes a unilateral choice to marry someone perceived to embody the prime threat to community safety. The crossover here between homes invaded and occupied by disproportionate military action and those invaded and occupied by disproportionate desire becomes apparent only when the other is revealed as lover, completing a movement always in motion from an other who can be tolerated, who can be secretly, inevitably desired, to an other who cannot be tolerated and must be banished once desire and the union for which it yearns are openly admitted. As black and minority ethnic individuals often experience, Anglo-Saxon goodwill can abruptly end when you turn up at their home or office, and the same can be said of inter-communal goodwill in Cyprus and Cypriot communities. Things change when the other becomes a reality knocking at the door.

This dynamic of exclusion structures the opening exchanges in *Othello*, where the clandestine marriage contradicts the processes Brabantio expects. Repeatedly accusing Othello of thievery and sorcery, Brabantio wonders how Desdemona could be 'So opposite to marriage that she shunned | The wealthy, curled darlings of our nation' yet, contrary to this seeming chastity, has 'Run from her guardage to the sooty bosom | Of such a thing' as Othello (1.2.67–8, 70–1). That Brabantio calls for Othello to be subject to the 'law, and course of direct session' (1.2.86) brings desire's excess under the forces of family and state, the twin agents of masculine 'guardage' or guardianship, laying bare the control fathers and father-figures have over what is and is not socially acceptable. So when it comes to light that Othello has indeed achieved what younger, wealthier and whiter suitors could not by winning the hand of Desdemona, the controlling authority of Venetian patriarchy, especially the reification of this authority in the family home, comes under threat. 'Signior, is all your family within?' Iago mischievously asks Brabantio. 'Are your doors locked?' adds Roderigo (1.1.83–4). As Brabantio cries foul at an abuse of convention that exposes the insecurity of the family home – 'O heaven, how got she out? O treason of the blood!' (1.1.167) – the controlling authority of Venetian patriarchy faces a simultaneous threat in Cyprus. The frantic opening act has, Cassio tells us, seen 'a dozen sequent messengers' relaying updates on the Ottoman fleet's advance to Cyprus via Rhodes. Meanwhile, 'The Senate hath sent about three several quests' to find Othello (1.2.38–47 (41, 46)), and the play's first confrontation occurs when the Duke's men seeking out Othello for immediate deployment in Cyprus meet Brabantio's men seeking to imprison him for his presumed bewitching of Desdemona. Amid all these dizzying comings and goings, the high-alert action of Act One conflates two core anxieties – the invasion and loss of Desdemona and the invasion and loss of Cyprus. And as this act draws to a close, Brabantio makes clear that Desdemona's sexual integrity and the military integrity of Cyprus are interchangeable, in a sarcastic response to the Duke's appeasement:

DUKE	The robbed that smiles steals something from the thief,
	He robs himself that spends a bootless grief.
BRABANTIO	So let the Turk of Cyprus us beguile,
	We lose it not so long as we can smile.
	(1.3.209–12)

Venice, in other words, should accept the loss of Cyprus with the same good grace with which Brabantio should apparently accept the loss of his daughter.

'What tell'st thou me of robbing? This is Venice.' These are Brabantio's words when Iago and Roderigo first rouse him from his slumber with the scandal of the Saggitary, where Desdemona and Othello are, presumably, drinking the night away.[5] 'My house', he cries, 'is not a grange' (1.1.104–5). Critics have often noted the sense of urban Venice as a safe house, a sanctuary of fairness and civility protected from outside, rural threats of incivility and injustice. Brabantio articulates his home the same way, as a microcosm of the *Serenissima*. In 1601, at about the same time as the initial composition of *Othello*, an English translation of Giovanni Botero's *The worlde* was published, in which Venice was described as 'an vntouched virgin [preserved] from the violence of any forreine inforcement' (1601: sig. N4ʳ [p. 95, misprinted as p. 97]). Unsurprisingly, then, the potential penetration of Desdemona doubles as an intrusion into Brabantio's home and the values his home, and by extension Venice, embodies. Desdemona's unconventional desire contravenes the interdependent laws of home and state. Despite the common Elizabethan and Jacobean stereotype of the sly, Machiavellian Italian, the Duke's eventual support legally endorses the secret marriage and, as many commentators have pointed out, indicates the perceived openness and fairness of Venice and the Venetian Signoria: William Thomas's *The historie of Italie* makes the point that in Venice, regardless of race or creed, 'thou arte free from all controllement' (1549: fol. 85ʳ), while Gasper Contarini, in Lewes Lewkenor's 1599 translation of

The commonwealth and gouernment of Venice, described how non-Venetians were welcomed into the higher echelons of society if 'they had beene dutifull towardes the state, or els had done vnto them some notable seruice' (1599: 18). Desdemona's rebellious desires thus cause a schism between the normally unified voices of father and paternal state, driving a wedge between the openness Thomas and Contarini identify and the opposite, uncompromised chastity of national borders sexualized by Botero's text. Our newly endorsed newlyweds are inevitably removed from Venice, exorcising from the central reservations of power the threat they embody to the home, the threat they embody to desire's appropriate and standard masculine coordinates. Desdemona is banished from the family home by Brabantio; Othello receives the military commission that removes him from Venice and takes Desdemona with him.

And where do we turn now? Where do we turn when we are thrust from the safety and certainty of the Venetian home, from homogeneous identity and safe, controllable sexuality? If the Venetian core feels threatened by an otherness it creates, by alien desires it itself holds and alien figures it itself has invited, then Cyprus is the site to which these monstrosities are expelled. It is a site where modern-day transgressions also threaten home and nation alike, where political disputes are distilled to domestic ones. And it is a site where narratives of transgression have always abounded. *Othello* has often been considered a play about turning: from love to jealousy, intimacy to murder, Christian to Turk. To turn Turk, to convert to Islam like Grimaldi in Philip Massinger's *The Renegado* and Ward in Robert Daborne's *A Christian Turn'd Turk*, constitutes an alarming hazard to the Christian certainties of early modern Europe. The turn to Cyprus in *Othello* would have pushed that particular button hard for a Jacobean audience well aware that the island *had already* turned Turk, famously becoming an infidel site home to the lasciviousness and brutality associated with the Muslim Ottomans, with the East, with the margins of Europe and the roads beyond. With the scandal of the Saggitary exposed, with the irregular prospect of their chiaroscuro love-making raised, Aphrodite's sex-drenched island becomes home to the radical newlyweds in much the same way that Venetian undesirables were forced to make it, and in particular the underpopulated Famagusta that still hosts Othello's Tower, their home.[6]

There are two aspects of Cyprus we can be pretty sure were common knowledge in early modern England. First, that it was an island much warred over. Knolles dedicated some sixty pages to these wars in *The generall historie of the Turkes* from 1603, which, given the details Shakespeare seems to have taken from this text, would fix the completion of *Othello* to 1603 or even 1604, the first year in which the Office of the Revels mentions a performance of 'The Moor of Venis' by 'Shaxberd'. When the action turns to Cyprus, audiences watching this latest work by 'Shaxberd' would have expected on-stage battles and brutal deaths due to their familiarity with the Cyprus Wars and the famously gruesome fate of Marco Antonio Bragadin. Referred to by Knolles as 'Bragadinus' and not to be confused with the Cypriot-born conman Marco Bragadino, who falsely claimed to be his son, Bragadin (or Bragadino) was disfigured, skinned alive and finally torn limb from limb by the Ottomans when Famagusta fell. Bragadin's harrowing ordeal sealed Ottoman victory with a gory punctuation point. English interest in these final events in particular was widespread and went right to the top: William Malim's translation of the eye-witness account by Martinengo, who was enslaved by the Ottomans in Famagusta before escaping, was produced for Robert Dudley, Earl of Leicester and personal favourite of Elizabeth I. Malim's gushing dedicatory epistle points out that the limitlessly talented Earl was already 'well acquainted with [the] Italian copy' (Martinengo 1572: sig. A4ʳ).

The second aspect of common knowledge regarding Cyprus was that it was home to the morally ambivalent pagan cult of Aphrodite, in whose name fathers, as Stephen Batman's translation of Bartholomaeus's *De Proprietatibus Rerum* puts it, offered their daughters 'to such straungers as came into the

Countrye, to bée by them deflowred, and afterwarde (with the game so gotten) married the[m] to husbands' (Bartholomaeus 1582: fol. 221ᵛ). Arthur Golding's hugely influential translation of Ovid's *Metamorphoses* presented Aphrodite herself, in the Westernized guise of Venus, as a deity of unchecked sexual passions from her first appearance in Book IV. Tipped off by the all-seeing Sun, Venus's husband, Vulcan, traps her in a net with her lover, Mars, much to the amusement of the onlooking gods, one of whom 'Did wish that he himselfe also were shamed in that sort' (Ovid 1567: 46). Did Shakespeare have this moment of bawdy adultery in mind when Iago, on seeing Cassio and Desdemona hold hands, promises their downfall 'With as little a web as this' (2.1.168)? Was he also thinking of the graver, more violent, backstory that Ovid gives in Book X, in which Venus forces the women of Amathus into prostitution and turns their men into wild bullocks as punishment for the sacrificial killing of foreigners at Jove's altar (Ovid 1567: 127)? In this context, *Othello* presents *Cyprus*, more so than Venice, as a place where domestic affairs and military affairs are symbiotic, where sex and death come together. Maybe, after all, Shakespeare was thinking more carefully about Cyprus than we have assumed. Maybe, after all, Shakespeare saw that Cyprus, contested and then lost, paradoxically associated with both purity and promiscuity, was the perfect place for Desdemona to step ashore just like Aphrodite. The perfect place for Desdemona to be whored and then killed.

Act Two

CASSIO   O, behold,
      The riches of the ship is come on shore:
      You men of Cyprus, let her have your knees!
                                     (2.1.82–4)

For so much of Act One, *Othello* points us away from Venice and towards Cyprus, towards the warred-over island of Aphrodite, goddess of love and lasciviousness, yet not once in the entire play do we hear any mention of Aphrodite or her more common Roman guise, Venus. 'A strange oversight', says Arden editor E. A. J. Honigmann on the matter, and little else, encapsulating in three words the flimsy treatment in *Othello* criticism of Venus's seeming absence ([1997] 2014: 11). This apparent omission has added grist to the mill of those for whom, as one critic put it in a moment of typical institutional neglect, Cyprus represents little more than the 'neutrality of a military fortress' (Mendonça 1968: 36). Such assessments discount urgent fears of proto-racial and religious transformation, fears Shakespeare stirred by adding the historical disputes Cinthio's *Hecatommithi* left out. What if, in fact, Shakespeare's omission of Venus was deliberate? What if it was a considered move by an experienced playwright managing the expectations raised by this setting rather than an easily dismissed act of carelessness? What if there was no omission at all?

As soon as the action turns to Cyprus in Act Two, the tone of *Othello* becomes overtly sexual. The 'wars are done' (2.1.20) as the wild seas destroy the Turkish fleet and the play switches emphasis from the Cyprus Wars to the ritual prostitution and sacrificial violence associated with the island's goddess. Golding's translation of *The Metamorphoses* preserves the titillating yet threatening mythological history familiar to Shakespeare and his audience: Cyprus was a place where, in Venus's name, 'the blood of strau[n]gers was spilled' and a dangerous climate of unchecked lust bred children 'voyd of grace' (Ovid 1567: 127, 128). So strong were the connections with an unbridled sexuality hazardous and alluring in equal measure that they formed everyday speech: 'Cypria' was an alternative name for Venus, while the adjective 'Cyprian' signified the island and its supposed amorousness, hence John Marston's reference to 'Cyprian dalliance' in the third of his satirical poems (Marston 1598b: sig. C8^v). In Thomas Dekker's *Old Fortunatus*, the flirtatious exchange between Andelocia, son to the Famagustan Fortunatus, and the English Agripyne plays on these connections. 'Tis the fashion of vs Cypriots, both men and women, to yéeld at first assault', explains Andelocia. Agripyne responds that 'either your women are very black, & are glad to be sped, or your men very fond, & wil take no denial' (Dekker 1600: sig. G1^v). Echoed by the quayside verbal horseplay between Desdemona and Iago on things black and sexual, this exchange turns on perceptions of 'Cyprian dalliance'. Robert Allot's poetry compendium *England's Parnassus* has a section dedicated to Venus in which John Harrington's poem 'Of Cyprus' celebrates the island as 'lustfull, (for dame *Venus* meete) [. . .] With wanton damsels walking in each street, | Inuiting men to pleasure and repast' (Allot 1600: 353). Cyprus as a site of transgression, and Venus as the representative of that transgressive tendency, were significations built into the language of Shakespeare's world.

This trope was part of the visual landscape too. Never mentioned, Venus nevertheless haunts the play from the moment Desdemona arrives 'upon the foaming shore' (2.1.11), a visual replay of the Cyprian goddess's mythical birth that pre-empts the sex and sacrificial death to come. With Othello's ship still negotiating the storm-tossed Mediterranean, Iago's salacious teasing of Desdemona clarifies, if clarification were needed, that we are now in a dangerous realm of lustful acts that even 'fair and wise ones do' (2.1.141–2 (142)). Far from being overlooked, the goddess has been there all along.

Alan C. Dessen has eloquently focused attention on a 'theatrical vocabulary [...] lost or blurred to us today' but shared by early modern playwrights, players and audiences (1995: 11). For Dessen, this visual vocabulary can be recovered through the examination of stage directions, which deepen our understanding of what theatregoers would have seen at London's playhouses and also reveal how sudden entrances, lingering exits and the use of props constituted a set of dramatic conventions key to fleshing out onstage action. We do not need to go as far as the play's marginalia to find something similar operating in *Othello*: the mythology and history of Cyprus resided not just in the words spoken by the players – in Iago's subtle reference to the nets of Vulcan or the repeated link between conflict and sexual transgression that makes adultery an 'office' (1.3.386) – but in the visual action those words described. Visual action tapped into a collective *cultural* vocabulary shared by Shakespeare, his fellow actors and their audience. Martha Ronk cites emblems, iconography and heraldry as instances of how physical symbols or set pieces carried a weight on the early modern stage difficult for modern audiences and readers to fully appreciate. Ronk explains that in the iconography of the play Desdemona is 'reified as whore or adored idol of love' (2005: 61). However, Ronk's analysis misses the most obvious iconographic allegory in the play: the immediate visual connection between Desdemona and Venus.

Desdemona's arrival is deified, aligned with love and sex, and greeted by the bended knees of worship. As Cyprus awaits her coming, a group of Cypriot gentleman – apparently 'they say nothing; they do not matter' (Hibbard 1968: 42) – are in discussion with incumbent governor Montano when Cassio's ship comes in. The lieutenant prepares the locals for their meeting with Othello's wife by describing her as a painstakingly crafted masterpiece who 'paragons description and wild fame [...] And in th'essential vesture of creation | Does tire the inginer' (2.1.61–5). Putting it simply, she's better than art, even if the artist is God. The deadly storm that disperses the advancing Turkish fleet will part, 'letting go safely by | The divine Desdemona' (2.1.68–73 (72–3)) and, as she steps on to Cypriot sands, Cassio demands genuflection: 'You men of Cyprus, let her have your knees!' In a culture preoccupied, even obsessed, with classical mythology, the common myth of Venus's creation by, as Shakespeare's colourful literary rival Robert Greene put it, 'the foame of the sea' (1585: sig. F4ᵛ) was not exactly secret or privileged knowledge that needed literal spelling out: Desdemona's disembarkation on Cypriot sands was powerfully emblematic, a living, breathing reminder of the pagan worship of Venus, establishing an immediately visible connection between the play's ill-fated heroine and the goddess's passionate vices.

The most scandalous of these passionate vices was the affair with Mars that saw the two lovers shamed before the gods. This episode in Book IV of *The Metamorphoses* seems to have made a profound and lasting impression on Shakespeare. Venus recounts the ribald mythological adultery during her desperate seduction of Adonis in *Venus and Adonis* (*VA*, ll. 97–114), Shakespeare's first publication, and it resurfaces again in *Antony and Cleopatra* (*AC*, 1.5.16–19). It was a common theme throughout the period too, as in the poem in *England's Parnassus* by 'D. Lodge' – presumably Thomas Lodge – that offers a stock description of 'Her louely locks her bosome hanging downe, | Those nets that first insnard the God of warre' (Allot 1600: 356). In *Othello*, Iago fashions a similar trap for his prey. When Othello arrives in Cyprus, he once more reminds us that 'our wars are done, the Turks are drowned'. The subsequent courtesy to Desdemona that she 'shall be well desired here in Cyprus' (2.1.201, 203) doubles, suggests Steven Doloff, as a 'veiled wink at Venus's association with the island and [. . .] its reputed amorous customs' (2000: 82), gently refocusing our attention from the off-stage Turkish fleet to the off-stage conjugal bed.[1] 'That profit's yet to come 'tween me and you', says Othello, with a twinkle in his eye, as the pair exit with great ceremony. 'Good night' (2.3.10–11). It should be.

Paying customers watching 'The Moor of Venis' in the early seventeenth century, from the groundlings to the jewellery-rattlers in the gods, would have known that any military celebrations were worryingly premature given the eventual Venetian capitulation. If history accounted for this sense of foreboding, Ovidian mythology dooms the sexual promise. Golding's *Metamorphoses* describes the moment Vulcan traps Venus and her lover Mars in a net 'more fine than any handwarpe oofe | Or that whereby the Spider hanges in sliding from the roofe' (Ovid 1567: 46). Shakespeare reproduces these warps and woofs when Iago vows to weave a web that will 'ensnare as great a fly as Cassio' (2.1.168–9), a vow he fulfils thanks to another woven object – the handkerchief. The first thread weft in the defamation of Desdemona swiftly follows the excited departure of the newlyweds when the fight between Cassio and Montano, deviously orchestrated by Iago, breaks out. In *Venus and Adonis*, the Cypriot setting is not mentioned until the goddess's silver doves return her to the sanctuary of Paphos in the very last stanza (*VA*, ll. 1189–94); the tale and its location were so ingrained in the cultural vocabulary that Shakespeare could forego unnecessary explication. Similarly, *Othello* never needs mention Venus by name for her presence to be felt in her fabled birthplace.

Not mentioning her by name could well have been a quite deliberate ploy. Venus appears explicitly throughout the rest of the Shakespearean canon. Occasionally, she is conventionally associated with beauty and romance, as with Iachimo's repentant testimony in *Cymbeline* that uses her as the paragon of womanhood (*Cym*, 5.5.153–68), or when Aaron the Moor, plotting the death of Bassanius and Lavinia's brutal rape in *Titus Andronicus*, tells his lover, Tamora, that 'though Venus govern your desires, | Saturn is dominator over mine' (*Tit*, 2.2.30–1). That anyone in a play so sensationally gory as *Titus Andronicus*, let alone the revenge-driven Tamora, could represent moderation, betrays both the irony of Aaron's comparison and any notion of Venus as wholesome. In a way less apparent to modern-day consumers of Shakespeare used to a clean-cut goddess of beauty and monogamous love, the name of Venus invoked threatening, orgiastic excess as well as dreamy-eyed romance. Perhaps the most concise example of Venus's perceived licentiousness comes in *Much Ado About Nothing*, when Claudio, falsely believing Hero unfaithful, denounces her as 'more intemperate in your blood | Than Venus, or those pamper'd animals | That rage in savage sensuality' (*MA*, 4.1.58–60). To the early modern mind, then, Venus was far from the comforting vessel of mainstream love and devotion peddled today by the Cypriot Tourism Organization, most conspicuously in the form of the Venus de Milo that adorns their marketing material. Shakespeare and his contemporaries would have imagined a more complex, more sensual and more pornographic goddess, one who at Paphos breathed life into Pygmalion's statue so that he could ravish her. She was, as Marston put it in *The Metamorphosis of Pygmalion's Image*, the 'sacred Queene of sportiue dallying [. . .] Whose kingdome rests in wanton reuelling' (1598a: 12). Shakespeare himself had helped reinforce this image.

In *Antony and Cleopatra*, Enobarbus describes Cleopatra, an amoral and highly sexual quasi-deity, resplendent on her barge, as 'O'erpicturing that Venus where we see | The fancy outwork nature' (*AC*, 2.2.210–11). Eighteenth-century editor Lewis Theobald believed Shakespeare had a specific picture in mind here – 'that fine Picture of *Venus* done by *Apelles*' (Theobald 1733: 242). Although such specificity is unlikely, Shakespeare clearly connected the generic and widely available image of Venus emerging from the sea, exemplified by Apelles's mosaic, with passion, luxury and indulgence. *Venus and Adonis* cites Diana as the cool model of chastity (*VA*, ll. 723–5), something Shakespeare repeats in *Cymbeline* by decorating the bedroom of the chaste Imogen with Diana's picture. Venus is Diana's hot, passionate counterpoint: 'Graze on my lips, and if those hills be dry, | Stray lower, where the pleasant fountains lie', she urges Adonis in typically forthright fashion (*VA*, ll. 233–4). *Othello* works hard to convince us of Desdemona's credentials as a bona fide manifestation of the virgin goddess Diana. Brabantio insists that she was against marriage, Othello calls her 'as fresh | as Dian's visage' (3.3.389–90), and Iago concedes that 'chaste dames even thus, | All guiltless, meet reproach' (4.1.46–7), all of which offset any connection between her and the licentiousness of Venus. Even the mention of Venus's son, Cupid, comes when Othello makes clear his own chaste intentions by assuring the senate that, should Desdemona accompany him, the erotic sting of the archer's arrows will not 'corrupt and taint' the business of war (1.3.268–76 (273)).[2]

On closer inspection, the 'oversight' appears more like a deliberate exclusion, one based on the connections Shakespeare's audience were likely to make. Venus's omission from the lexicon of love and desire in *Othello* ensures our conviction that the accusation of infidelity is false. Any doubt or suspicion about Desdemona's chastity would transform Othello's brutality from unjust to disproportionate, robbing the ending of its excruciating needlessness. Iago would be little more than a glorified tell-tale. Psychological critiques have often sought to explain the ease with which Iago seduces Othello, from A. C. Bradley's early view of Othello as 'unusually open to deception' (1957: 151) to Eric S. Mallin's recent vision of a flawed husband whose 'considerable insecurities' are down to personal and sexual imperfections (2012: 43). These psychological profiles of Othello fail to acknowledge Cyprus as a realm of sexual transgression – a realm of debauchery, ritual prostitution and sacrificial murder, all for Venus's sake. When the Herald proclaims the marriage celebrations, he orders 'each man to what sport and revels his addiction leads him' and declares that 'All offices are open' (2.2.5–6, 8), bringing together all the vectors of Cypriot dalliance:

Bartholomaeus's tales of prostitution; the atmosphere of free love encapsulated by the poems of *England's Parnassus*; Pygmalion's sex-slave statue; Iago's symbiosis of conflict and congress that sees military 'office' performed between the sheets; the murder Othello considers a 'sacrifice' (5.2.65). Desdemona is chaste, we know this, but that her chastity can be doubted owes much to a backdrop in which wantonness is expected even from the innocent, a backdrop as familiar to Shakespeare's audience as it must be to the island's governor and returning hero, Othello.

*

In the age of Empire, these early modern myths of dark sexual liaisons resurfaced in colonialist rhetoric. At first, in the relatively stable years of British rule, Venus was depicted as a welcoming, acquiescent goddess, from *Punch* magazine draping her in a British flag to greet the first High Commissioner, Sir Garnet Wolseley (*Punch*, 3 August 1878, 46), to Sir Richmond Palmer, governor between 1933 and 1939, pompously explaining that the island's people, just like its goddess, 'expect to be ruled, and, in fact, prefer it' (Palmer 1939: quoted in Given 2002: 423). The island, like Venus, was asking for it. This concept of easy dominance over a feminized, pliant and available Cyprus coincided with a boom in prostitution. Urbanization and the high number of British soldiers increased demand beyond what the old-fashioned bordellos could satisfy. The critical mass of young men willing to pay for sex transformed Nicosia's cabaret industry into the Middle East's most infamous, while the colonial government's taste for the house girls earned it the nickname of 'The Cabaret Government of Cyprus' (Constantinou 2013: 286). One soldier who carried out his national service in Cyprus recalls how those lower down the chain of command also indulged in extra-curricular activities:

> *We were in Kermia Camp, which was a tented camp on the outskirts of Nicosia, to the west. And almost immediately*

the rioting started between the Turks and the Greeks in Nicosia. I was a brand new subaltern with a brand new platoon [. . .] I had to get used to a platoon of 30 men, a mixture of regulars and national servicemen, most of whom didn't want to be there. There was homesickness. These were eighteen-year-olds, nineteen-year-olds, first time they'd been away. There was the hard drinking side. One of the patrols we had to do was in Ledra Street, which was the main street in Nicosia. We were on observation duty with a few of my platoon, looking down, and I couldn't understand why they all kept disappearing for half an hour or so. I was very naïve in those days. We were on top of a brothel.

Personal interview with the author, January 2015

When, in the early 1950s, the actors' and performers' union, Equity, warned dancers against working on what the *Daily Mail* euphemistically called the 'sociable island', the matter for concern was that young women were forced to encourage customers to buy drinks (*Daily Mail*, 6 August 1953). Even this enacted colonial sensibility, as in the case of six British dancers who refused to act as hostesses because 'the girls objected to mix except with their own friends, generally British and New Zealand airmen' (*Daily Mail*, 5 August 1953); the British women chose not to serve Cypriot men. A similar case was resolved when four dancers were allowed to move to the Acropole Hotel, which housed the Key Club, a popular haunt with British officers (*Daily Mail*, 4 July 1959). As Angelo C. Constantinou puts it in his study of the legal issues behind the modern sex industry in Cyprus, 'Aphrodite and her descendants were meant to be the receiving end of control, dominance and sexual penetration [. . .] but never the other way round' (2013: 287). Native practices were okay for the colonists, but not for the natives.

During the emergency years of 1955 to 1959, the EOKA movement reclaimed Aphrodite as propagandist proof of the 'primordial Greekness' of Cyprus, justifying both *enosis* and the European right to democratic self-determination. Both imperialists and Greek nationalists were now making 'Aphrodite speak in support of their opposed political ideologies' (Papadakis 2006: 239). With British military and civilian deaths racking up due to EOKA's guerrilla warfare and with growing numbers of British women employed as cabaret girls, the issue of 'improper relations', previously overlooked by the British press, became a sudden concern. Despite colonial officials and soldiers propping up the sex industry to such an extent that cabarets sat alongside government and military buildings on EOKA's bombing lists, these exploitative habits were still 'local customs' (*Daily Mail*, 4 July 1959). Just as it was in Shakespeare's day, Cyprus was once more perceived as a place of violence and habitual prostitution. In this climate of colonial fear and desire, the colonial government cast aside the Hellenistic vision of Aphrodite seen in *Punch* and hijacked by EOKA – a Greco-Roman paragon of acquiescent white femininity similar to those painted by realist artists of the Nazi regime such as Adolf Ziegler and Ernst Liebermann. The Mesopotamian version of the goddess, Ashtart or Astarte, was taken up instead. This oriental manifestation was peddled as degenerate, a symbol of the moral and genetic corruption that rendered Cypriots unable, in their mongrel diversity, to govern themselves with any unity (see Given 2002: 419–23; Papadakis 2006: 239–40). The problem with Cyprus became miscegenation.

In early colonial literature the various manifestations of the goddess were, as Elizabeth Lewis's *A Lady's Impression of Cyprus in 1893* puts it, a product of 'the natural meeting-place of east and west'. For Lewis, the people of Cyprus were more like Astarte than Aphrodite or Venus: they were absolutely oriental, 'slothful, mendacious, voluptuous', and the two major communities could not be recognized, or separated out, as Greeks or Turks (1894: 117, 202). Traveller and historian William Hepworth Dixon was of a similar mind: 'In blood and race both men are Cypriotes' (1879: 20). Sixty years after Lewis and Dixon, the colonial government's transformation of Aphrodite into her Mesopotamian incarnation became 'proof' that oriental Cypriots could not self-govern given the doubt over a stable, pure or European Cypriot self. Moreover, the composite goddess who for Lewis and Dixon signified the difference of Cypriots *from* Greeks and Turks became a signifier of their incompatible, ungovernable differences from each other *as* Greeks and Turks. A political reality to mirror this mythological impurity was also put in place, a two-pronged approach that consisted of tackling the 'intermingling of the two races' and polarizing Greek Cypriots and Turkish Cypriots, a process that would have to be 'artificially induced [. . .] over a period of ten years or more' (The National Archives [TNA], FCO 141/4363: 'Partition').[3] The establishment of the Republic of Cyprus in 1960 at the end of the emergency years merely delayed, until 1974, a division thrashed out by Britain, Greece and Turkey as the battles with EOKA raged. To facilitate the burgeoning ideology of division, the colonial government constructed Cyprus as a land of distinct races. In terms of propagandist justification for this ideology, where early colonial travellers imagined Astarte as an allegory of oriental *diversity* in Cyprus, the colonial government abandoned the Aphrodite of Hellenism or her Roman doppelganger and propagated the idea of mismatched races whose incompatibility was demonstrated by Astarte's dispersed, pan-Middle Eastern story. Astarte's qualities were used to support a diametrically opposed construction of the island's population from that found in the travelogues written sixty years before.

It is precisely the nefarious notion of an adulteration that cannot hold, of an interracial impurity or instability destined to fall apart, of an unavoidable partition to be violently managed, that Iago turns on Othello. He does so in surroundings known for the adultery of Venus and the deviant offspring from her affair with Mars, the intersex Hermaphroditus who is 'but halfe a man' (Ovid 1567: 44). Desdemona's perverted choice will, Iago warns, produce descendants who 'neigh' (1.1.111). It must, Iago warns, inevitably lead to the collapse of the marriage; it is 'Foul disproportion, thoughts unnatural' from which Desdemona will 'happily repent' (3.3.237, 242). There seems to be so much to celebrate when the Venetian ships first dock: the invading Ottomans have been defeated by the tempest; Desdemona has arrived safely, the men of Cyprus suggestively on their knees for her as if for their sea-born goddess. Othello disembarks, inviting all there to celebrate the end of conflict and the start of wedlock: 'Come, let us to the castle' (2.1.200). But this journey from quayside to castle proves a fateful one. With the promise of a silk handkerchief, Iago will soon convince Othello that Desdemona's perverted choice has in fact already borne bitter fruit. This seduction, the great temptation scene in which Iago entices Othello into composing the narrative of Desdemona's infidelity himself, doubles as an interrogation, an inquisition that sets Othello 'on the rack' (3.3.338). Home to Venus, home to violence, Cyprus also becomes home to Othello's torture.

Act Three: Part One

IAGO O monstrous world! Take note, take note, O world,
To be direct and honest is not safe.
            (3.3.380–1)

Once the threat of miscegenation has been expelled from Venice to the more apposite site of Cyprus, and once the debauched atmosphere of violence and sexual conflict has been established on the island, Iago begins to weave his Ovidian web. His machinations trouble the very idea of honesty so that trusting it becomes unsafe: those who present themselves as the proponents of 'truth' as a value are precisely the ones you cannot trust. He takes his first victim when he lures Cassio into the drunken fight with Montano, the previous governor of Cyprus. Then, in the central scene of *Othello*, he exploits his meticulously manufactured reputation for 'exceeding honesty' (3.3.262) to convince Othello that Desdemona and Cassio are lovers; Desdemona's petitioning on the disgraced Cassio's behalf is spun as the initial evidence of their adultery. To what extent does the Cypriot setting inform this crucial exchange? Did Shakespeare expect the island's libidinous mythology to add some credence to Iago's fanciful image of Desdemona as a yearning, writhing vixen ready to explode? Did the common belief, reiterated by Pierre d'Avity in *The estates, empires, & principallities of the world*, that Cypriot brides-to-be 'came vpon certaine daies to the sea shore, to present themselues to the first stranger that would vse them for money' (1615: 1003) make Othello's susceptibility to the fantasy of infidelity plausible? After all, Desdemona disembarks to the sea shore and presents herself to none other than Cassio; for Shakespeare's audience, few places in the known world would fit the bill for unexpected dalliances as well as the home of Venus. Or did the titillating legends and literatures swirling around the play's margins heighten, rather than justify, the tragedy of this scene by juxtaposing Desdemona's innocence with a folkloric aura of unchecked sexuality? Whether the backdrop corroborates or counters the false claims, the exchange between Iago and Othello remains heavily layered with sexual motifs right up until Iago's final, quasi-matrimonial promise that he is Othello's 'for ever' (3.3.482). This palimpsest of secret desires and half-spoken accusations has come to be known as the temptation scene, uniting the intense sexual anxiety with Iago's allegorical role as silver-tongued serpent. These biblical skills of rhetoric – a slow-burn paralipsis that emphasizes Desdemona's indiscretion by seeming to ignore it and a coy taciturnity that gradually cranks up the pressure on Othello – have seen Iago compared to every linguistic trickster imaginable: the canny Devil in mystery plays; the quibbling figure of Vice in morality plays; the quick-witted Venetian mountebanks who hawked quack medicines (Spivack 1958: 424; Scragg 1968; Weimann and Bruster 2008: 26; Mirabella 2011). But this seductive taciturnity has a less studied flip side.

At the moment he considers Othello caught, Iago's tight-lipped modus operandi becomes a fierce, aggressive loquacity. Good cop becomes bad cop, turning the *tête-à-tête* from a provocation to what Othello calls a 'torture' (3.3.371). For me, Iago's transition brings *Othello* and Cyprus together in an even more radical way than the prostituting legacy of Venus colouring events for theatregoers in early seventeenth-century London. As seduction becomes interrogation, Iago successfully plays the stand-up guy twisted by a monstrous world, a schema repeated by the British interrogators in Cyprus who abused my father during the emergency years. In the island's colonial torture cells, trusting those who claimed to be direct and honest could be hazardous in the extreme, an echo of Othello's dilemma. An echo I keep hearing.

*

The passage to the abuses of the emergency years opens in Nicosia on 12 July 1878 as the Union Jack was raised. Archbishop Sophronios III welcomed the British on behalf of all Orthodox and Muslim inhabitants. There was no mention of Greeks or Turks; it was religion that defined Cypriot identity. Built into nineteenth-century British understandings of Cyprus were notions of classical Greece and the foundations of Christianity. Culturally, if not geographically, the island was expected to be a European site infused with the spirit of Richard I, the Islamophobia of the Crusades and the anti-Turk scaremongering of early modern Turk plays. Even military evaluations of the island's naval worth repeatedly cited the obdurate, if doomed, resistance to the Ottoman assaults of the sixteenth century. Those first officials who arrived, and the travel writers such as Elizabeth Lewis and William Hepworth Dixon who would soon follow, found their expectations to be way off the mark. The fierce enmity between Islam and Christianity that characterized proto-colonial mercantile struggles throughout southern Europe, North Africa and the Levant, a struggle for which Cyprus was a major bellwether, had largely dissipated. This was a time when 'Orthodox and Muslim Cypriots shared a language, folklore, economic and social hardships, and intermarried' (Varnava 2009: 155). This was not *Othello*.

British officials soon created a more familiar place by applying the 'door bolt' to this *zona mista*. Faced with a people they could not racially categorize on an island that escaped the hardening religious and cultural definitions of Orient and Occident, the British took action. They separated church and state, created a legislature divided proportionally between Orthodox and Muslim council members, and identified those represented by the council members along distinct ethnic lines.

Although these were standard British political frameworks, under them Cypriots were no longer Cypriots: they were Greeks or Turks, and the foundations had been laid for one of the Mediterranean's most problematic *catenaccio* points. It would take seventy-seven years, but the administrative structures of modernity created an 'imagined ethnic identity' (Varnava 2009: 152) that would reproduce the anti-Turkish sentiment of the Cyprus Wars in the form of a radical Hellenism turned against British rule. If the colonial Cyprus Government was Dr Frankenstein, EOKA was the monster it created.[1]

The violent challenge to colonial rule began with EOKA's first declaration, a written statement that appeared on 1 April 1955 to coincide with a series of coordinated bomb attacks on British military and communications sites. Signed by EOKA leader Georgios Grivas, the statement demanded liberation from British rule, which was seen as the first step to *enosis*, union with Greece. This first declaration represents the clearest stand-alone example of how the traditional signifiers of Hellenic identity were internalized in Cyprus in the colonial period. Grivas signed the typed statement with his nom de guerre 'Digenis', a Beowulf-style hero of the Acritic songs, epic poems inspired by medieval Arab-Byzantine wars. Added to this was an emotive call to arms: in bold capitals were the words 'Η ΤΑΝ Η ΕΠΙ ΤΑΣ' – 'with it or on it' – the apocryphal send-off Spartan wives gave their soldier husbands as they left for the Battle of Thermopylae: return victorious with your shield or dead on it. A nationalist fight to the death was promised, and the candlelit shrine at Nicosia's National Struggle Museum for Greek Cypriots who lost their lives in this fight proves the promise was kept.

This Greco-Byzantine mosaic of Hellenism in full colour found its apotheosis in Grigoris Afxentiou, EOKA's second-in-command. Disguised as an Orthodox monk, he refused to surrender to the British troops surrounding his mountain hideout. Urged to give up his arms, Afxentiou quoted the defiant words believed to be Leonidas's last as the Persians closed in on their Pyrrhic victory: 'Μολών λαβέ' – 'come and take them'.[2] Displayed on the wall near the shrine of the martyrs sits a congratulatory message published in the British press from Field Marshal John Harding, governor of Cyprus at the time, to the regiment who burned Afxentiou alive in his cave. Below Harding's message sits an anonymously penned panegyric, 'The Ballad of Gregory Afxentiou', which strikes an ambivalent tone in its celebration of both the soldiers' success and Afxentiou's resistance: 'For the regiment gained new honour | When sixty men killed one.' If *Othello* helps set, and then problematize, an early caricature of fanatical Muslims, the inspiration Grivas and the lionized Afxentiou took from the resistance of European Hellenism to the inhuman assaults of Asia Minor created fanatical Christians. The battles of antiquity and the Cyprus Wars of Shakespeare's time were used to unite Greek nationalism with religious zealotry. Not all who supported independence shared this zealotry, but it did mean that membership of the organization came exclusively from the island's Greek-speaking community and, in the main, harboured a frenzied commitment to the Church-backed ideology of *enosis*. In Cyprus, the Christians have been the ones fighting a holy war.[3]

In quick response to EOKA's bombing campaign, the colonial government passed the Detention of Persons Law in July 1955. This gave the governor the right to detain indefinitely any person suspected of membership of, or who in any way aided or promoted, organizations committing 'acts of violence directed to the overthrow by force or violence of the Government' (TNA, FCO 141/4321: *Cyprus Gazette* no. 3839, 15 July 1955). Although clearly aimed at EOKA and used mainly against those thought to be active members, the Detention of Persons Law was used to detain others, including suspected communists.[4] If a detention order was suspended, or, in other words, a detainee was released without charge, they could still be subject to restrictions on employment, places of residence, articles of possession, association and communication with others, have a curfew imposed and be required to notify the authorities of his or her movements. For both the colonial government and their counterparts in Whitehall, EOKA were terrorists and any sympathizers were supporters of a terrorist organization. Nine EOKA men were officially executed, while colonial officers brutally abused those interrogated for information on the organization's activities. Male and female detainees were subject to beatings, whippings that included the use of chains, waterboarding, forced standing and electro-torture. As in Shakespeare's day, Cyprus was again a place of sexual proclivity and extreme violence. As in Shakespeare's day, the two were sometimes difficult to separate. During the four violent years of the emergency, my father's commitment to the cause of bulwarking Cyprus against threats from Asia Minor brought him to the attention of these officers. He would, like Othello, embark on a fateful journey to the castle.

*

I was first arrested at eighteen, the early hours of one morning on the way back from Kyrenia with some friends, about three hundred yards from my door on Kronos Street, Nicosia. The British had this law where they could arrest anyone under suspicion of involvement with EOKA and lock them up indefinitely. They took me and the others arrested that night to the Central Prisons in Nicosia first. I was number fourteen. Makis Yiorghallas, who later died in a battle, was number fifteen. They were converting Kyrenia Castle into a detention centre. When it was ready they moved us there as our numbers grew. They put me in the van. I remember the words: 'Straight to the castle.'

At the castle there were fifteen of us in one room. The smaller rooms had about six people. We were let out for fifteen minutes in the morning to walk around a bit, go to the toilet, and fifteen minutes in the evening. When the detention centre at Kokkinotrimithia was completed, Camp 'K' as they called it, I was moved there. Of the twenty-one months they held me, eighteen were spent here. I was never charged with anything.

The detention centre at Kokkinotrimithia was like a barrack, three dozen of us in a long room, like a dormitory room. There were over one thousand detainees. They built a smaller one at Pyla when this one was full too. We had a bit more freedom at Kokkinotrimithia. We were allowed visits once a week, though we had to post invitations. No one could visit without an invitation. There were books, so you could read a bit, and there was enough room outside to play volleyball, but not football, though we used to have a kind of kick-about anyway. When I was released, I was no longer involved with EOKA. I was not sure enosis was worth the price we were paying. I had a place at teacher-training college but, I don't know, I didn't feel like being in a classroom anymore. I had lost my job in the NAAFI accounts department when I was arrested. I got a new job and left it all behind.

After my release I had to be indoors between sunset and sunrise. One day, British officers came to check, and I wasn't there. I was summoned to the police station, and that's when I was imprisoned the second time. Three months in the Central Prisons for breaking curfew. There was one Irish, rough-looking type, who was sometimes on duty at night. Now, cigarettes were not allowed, but, when he thought everyone was asleep, he would walk past the cells and throw a cigarette in each one. He was okay. We would all share one cigarette between us, and because we only got a cigarette every two weeks or so, we'd get a buzz off just one puff.

The final time I was imprisoned was after an English civilian was shot dead. That same night British officers raided our house. Some kept me in the living room, searched the house, made a mess of my mother's bedroom. They took one of my younger brothers into the yard outside, and as I sat in the living room I could hear them beating him up. Each time they hit him, I could hear him cry out. I was twenty by now, he was seventeen.

I was on my own in a cell just about big enough to lie down in for twenty-eight days at Omorphita, a suburb of Nicosia between Kaimakli and Trakhona. It was the shortest spell I spent inside, but definitely the worst. There was this club, the Key Club, at the Acropole Hotel. Every night the British officers would go there, get pissed, come back after midnight and start their interrogations. From my cell I could hear the other prisoners being beaten. You'd go into the interrogation room, wearing nothing but your underpants, and they'd shine these bright, bright lights at you so that they could see you but you couldn't see them. They spoke in perfect Greek and they knew all about you: 'Tell us what you know, we'll send you to England where your brother and father are. We can help you. You can escape all this trouble.' In EOKA training they always told us to say 'No', nothing else, whether you knew anything or not, because if you gave them the slightest hint you would cooperate, they would never stop. You just took your beating, and then back to the cell. They wouldn't even allow me a change of underwear. I left there in blood-soaked underpants. English. 'Civilized'.

Everything postcolonial studies have tried to uncover and voice, the once untold, buried stories behind the vision of progress for the poor of the world, was summed up in two words. He spoke with a smile, or as close to one as the leathery skin of his Arab cowboy scowl allowed. He and all those young boys, so long ago, were already well aware that the testimony of the oppressed is judged according to different standards of truth than the testimony of the privileged. *English. 'Civilized'.*

*

OTHELLO	What dost thou think?
IAGO	Think, my lord?
OTHELLO	Think, my lord! By heaven, thou echo'st me As if there were some monster in thy thought Too hideous to be shown.

(3.3.107–11)

ACT THREE: PART ONE

If there was ever a morning when I woke up before my father, I don't remember it. He was always awake before dawn every day of the week and gone before the rest of us had opened our eyes. Returning from work late in the evening, he would fall asleep at the dinner table. The next day he would be up before dawn again. When he was unemployed for a while, he still beat the sun. And when he got a new job with different hours and some weekends free? Up before dawn every day of the week. And every morning the same routine: a cigarette, a crossword on the table, chair facing the kitchen window, beyond the kitchen window the darkness of Euston Road illuminated here and there by intermittent brake lights, flashing primers to the rush hour traffic that would prove too tardy to delay him. A muted dawn chorus from the window ledges or from the pavement trees. A tinny portable radio sitting on the table. The door always open or ajar. And there I would stand on the rare mornings I saw him, hesitating at the threshold of the room, at the threshold of the day and, without knowing why, reluctant to disturb his solitude.

One summer morning I walked out on to a veranda in Cyprus to the familiar sight of him sat at a table concentrating on his crossword, cigarette balanced on a glass ashtray, pen in hand and prehistoric radio crackling away, more white noise than news. He was retired and back where he felt he belonged, but some things had stayed the same. The sun was only just breaking through the pine trees on the eastern hills. We made a visit to Camp 'K' that day. As I drove, my mother told the story of how she met my father on a double date in a beachside Larnaca taverna. How he tried in vain to get her drunk on brandy. How she overheard him ask his friend whether they had enough to pay for all the empty bottles. In the early hours he dropped her back home in Nicosia and, if only to avoid disturbing her landlady, she agreed to a date in the Troodos Mountains. He arrived the next morning before dawn.

There was not much to see at Camp 'K'. A tree-lined stretch of tarmac dotted with commemorative tablets led from the entrance down to a commemorative plinth. White barracks were situated either side of the tarmac. A small piece of a shutter came off in my hand as I looked into the small, bare room that used to be my father's prison. The barrack that was once the officer's hall was now an empty visitor centre for schoolchildren. Presumably this visitor centre was used less and less, since a spirit of rapprochement gained momentum in the first decade of the new century under communist President Dimitris Christofias and his counterpart in the north, Mehmet Ali Talat, who together spoke of a diverse, but united, Cyprus beyond past troubles. Their ideal has become as muddled as we were when we left the camp, lost on one of my father's shortcuts, which always turn out to be a road that no longer exists, a road that now ends abruptly and sends you back the way you came. We went round and round one of the myriad suburbs that surround Nicosia. These new communities mark the startling, tourism-fuelled growth that followed the war of 1974 – the economic miracle, as it came to be known – each new settlement rearticulating, reinterpreting, the last as it boldly sweeps aside the dwindling landscape of pre-urban Cyprus. At another roundabout that led back the way we came, or off to an industrial zone, or on to a road only my father could remember, I asked what he thought now, in retrospect, about the emergency years. How did it *feel*? 'Feel?' What did it *mean*? 'Mean?' *Othello*, with its string of twisted recapitulations, might be an 'echo chamber' (Moisan 1991: 50), but we had just created our own. Perhaps we had reached the limit of how much he wanted to discuss. He was fine about it all. Others were not. Others died. Makis Yiorghallas died. A candle still shines for him in the National Struggle Museum. There was little more to add. Was I interrogating him now? Was he interrogating me? Who was asking whom what?

Stefan D. Keller points out that the rhetorical practice of anadiplosis – the repetition of the previous word or phrase – is most often employed by a single speaker. Shakespeare bucks this trend in the temptation scene by creating 'echo effects' between two speakers, Iago and Othello (2010: 404). Those with a Renaissance education in the classical trivium of rhetoric, grammar and logic may well have taken this unique deployment of anadiplosis as a clue to Iago's successful seduction of Othello. From a rhetorical perspective, they begin to speak as one.

> I was fine about it all. Others were not.
> Others were not, no.
> Others died.
> Others did die. Like Makis Yiorghallas.
> Yiorghallas. He recruited me.
> He recruited you? A candle still shines for him in the National Struggle Museum.
> It should, definitely.
> Definitely, yes.
> Ah well.
> Well.

Perhaps my father and I were not speaking at cross-purposes at all but also speaking as one. Perhaps we still are. That night, with friends and relatives, we sat on the veranda. We drank, like Iago claims the English drink, and discussed our trip to Camp 'K' until my father stood up, called over his German Pointer and asked me with a mischievous smile, 'What time do you want me to wake you tomorrow?' Even the Pointer seemed to get the joke.

The next morning: the veranda again. I had wanted a word or statement, a current repetition, however oblique, of a time and place that retained an unreachable kernel of mystery. I had wanted to locate some lingering remainder in the now from that time, a time otherwise inaccessible to me outside the reconstruction of it in writing. But when, in the end, would all the victims and protagonists of the troubles in Cyprus stop to reflect on what the conflicts they lived through 'mean'? When they were in a British cell? When EOKA crushed the skull of a loved one or TMT left them on a roadside with their severed genitals in their mouths? When Greek militia and Turkish bombs forced them from their homes? When they moved to new countries and started from scratch? And if they did reflect on the traumas, how would they speak of them? Georgio

Agamben identifies a paradox in Primo Levi's accounts of his incarceration at Auschwitz, where 'the survivors bore witness to something it is impossible to bear witness to' (Agamben 2005: 13). Only the dead can truly bear witness. *Others died.* Then again, a trace from the irretrievable past provides those of us who come after with the impetus to reimagine those events, understand them anew, reinvigorate them ethically.

As the sun began to rise and tentative cicada song began in the trees, it struck me that what I wanted had always been there, every early morning, in a guise not immediately recognizable. Maybe there are times when, consciously or not, your psyche does work through the past. Maybe right here, on a veranda surrounded by aromatic springtime freesias and wild poppies red in the field, looking out at the country you left or which left you, when everyone but the dog is sleeping, you think about it. Maybe this insomniac solitude is the trace, the remainder from long ago. By accident or by design my father could have been bearing witness all along, telling us how it felt and what it meant. *I was on my own.* The small cell just about big enough for him to lie down. *Back after midnight and start their interrogations.* The night at its pre-dawn darkest. *From my cell I could hear the other prisoners being beaten.* The underwear drenched in blood. *The early hours of one morning.* The sun yet to rise and tentative cicada song in the trees. And now, before you, the country you left or which left you. The prehistoric portable radio crackling away all night for company, more white noise than news, and still with you on the table as the sun breaks through the pine trees on the eastern hills. Is this a victory? Is it a defeat? What does Iago say when he knows Othello has been caught in his web of lies, knows Othello has been poisoned and irreversibly damaged by his torture chamber?

IAGO Not poppy nor mandragora
Nor all the drowsy syrups of the world
Shall ever medicine thee to that sweet sleep
Which thou owedst yesterday.
(3.3.333–6)

ACT THREE: PART ONE

*

As newspapers began to report allegations of torture and questions were asked in Parliament as to what the colonial Cyprus government was hiding, the treatment of detainees was explained away on the basis that it was the captured Cypriots who were products of a dishonest culture. A letter from the chief of staff in Cyprus to the Secretary of State for the Colonies, Alan Lennox-Boyd, from June 1957 describes 'a hard and bitter struggle between the forces of law and order and an utterly ruthless terrorist movement'. On the one side were terrorists with 'no tradition of truthfulness' and on the other 'policemen and soldiers brought up in a tradition of open dealing and keeping to the plain truth' (TNA, FCO 141/4310: 'Allegations of Ill-Treatment made against the Security Forces', 7 June 1957). The chief of staff's letter was in response to accusations against two captains, a case that piqued interest in Parliament. Repeated requests for information and clarification from Labour MP Francis Noel-Baker, for instance, aimed to establish whether the case revealed or repudiated 'stories of widespread atrocities'. Noel-Baker's interest, as well as an increasing number of journalists reporting allegations of torture, prompted Governor Harding to respond. He sent a confidential telegram to Lennox-Boyd with a general note on the allegations. In this, Harding describes the allegations as a 'smear campaign [. . .] designed to impress public opinion'. For Harding, the 'smear campaign' aimed to deter the proper interrogation of suspects who, in any case, 'pour out their stories with very little prompting' either because they are seeking leniency or due to low EOKA morale (TNA, FCO 141/4310: Letter from Francis Noel-Baker to Field Marshal Harding of 7 February 1956; Telegram 411 of 2 March 1957). The chief of staff's letter and Harding's telegram to Lennox-Boyd both whitewash the existence of torture; the two captains, Robin Linzee and Gerald O'Driscoll, had already been charged with assault and providing false evidence. A narrative of honesty versus dishonesty was built up, of British right-doing versus Cypriot wrong-doing.[5]

This narrative seeped into popular literature, too. Lawrence Durrell, press officer for the colonial government in the mid-1950s, perpetuated the stereotype of the dishonest Cypriot in his 1957 travelogue, *Bitter Lemons of Cyprus*, in which he criticized 'the tireless dissimulation and insincerity of the Mediterranean way of life' ([1957] 2000: 25). Ian Stuart Black's popular 1961 novel, *The High Bright Sun* – and the 1964 film adaptation – also pits its British hero, McGuire, against mendacious Cypriot antagonists. These Cypriot antagonists are deceptive, sexually aggressive, murderously violent or capture and unlawfully detain the heroine, Juno, practices acceptable when perpetrated by the roguish McGuire.[6] The interplay and exchange between cultural texts and ideological institutions, which has become a new historicist staple of Shakespeare studies, also applies to the colonial milieu: an iniquitous complicity existed between the sweeping generalizations of official colonial discourse and those of contemporary literature about Cyprus. Popular texts packaged the dogma of Levantine mendacity versus British sincerity for the general consumption of readers.

The appeal to straightforward honesty made by official discourse and popular literature also strikes a Shakespearean chord for me. It has a long dramatic tradition as a favoured strategy of the smart-talking stage trickster popularized by the medieval Devil or Vice figure that Shakespeare revamped for the early modern stage in the form of Iago. These figures always seem to offer help. *Tell us what you know, we'll send you to England where your brother and father are.* These figures, like that other great linguistic trickster, Richard III, serve their own aggressive, exploitative and malicious needs from beneath a veneer of respectability or honesty. A very English history of professed veracity reverberates in my ears when I hear Iago's ironic claim that 'Men should be what they seem' (3.3.129). When the seduction of Othello becomes interrogation, Iago successfully plays the stand-up guy doing what's best: 'I hope you will consider what is spoke | Comes from my love' (3.3.220–1). This schema of honest intentions simply misunderstood was repeated by British interrogators in Cyprus: *We can help you. You can escape all this trouble.* To be direct and honest may well be unsafe, but trusting those who claim to be the gatekeepers of truth and honesty is more so by a distance.

Act Three: Part Two

OTHELLO   'Tis true, there's magic in the web of it.
                                                    (3.4.71)

Where my father found assimilation to life in Britain difficult, a combination of the distrust beaten in to him and his relatively late arrival as an adult, my mother adapted quickly. Her father, employed to build roads by the colonial public works department at the age of eight, was one of the many Cypriots who fought in the British Army in the Second World War, following in the footsteps of his own father, a volunteer in the First World War. My mother was barely ten years old when her father moved the family to post-war London in search of work. So young, and so blonde, she soon overcame not knowing a word of English to become every bit the London girl, working in the West End for sixty years with a lingering accent that initially gave her provenance away and a surname that sealed the deal. These decades were interrupted briefly by a stay in Cyprus to reconcile one home with another, an interregnum that brought a husband back to London. Southampton Row, Covent Garden, Soho, Piccadilly – in the end she came to know these places far better than the pan-handle landscape of her receding childhood. The flats in a basement or above a shop in Old Compton Street or Shaftesbury Avenue, or the Fitzrovia streets in the tall, slender shadow of the great telecommunications tower – Maple Street, Cleveland Street, Warren Street – were home to family and friends from the same village. This was a pre-yuppie time when immigrants from Cyprus, Malta, Bangladesh and other countries of the Commonwealth could afford to live in Central London. She told me often of the overflowing baskets of pears that her father brought home to the West End from the orchards of Heathrow, the farms and market gardens rapidly disappearing as the construction sites of London Airport, as it was then known, continued to expand. While her father worked on those construction sites, her mother was in the factories of Bloomsbury and Euston, putting to good use the weaving and needlework skills key to everyday life back in the village.

The embroidered silk handkerchief derided as 'a trifle' in Thomas Rymer's notorious critique of *Othello* (Rymer 1693: 86–146 (140)) has become a staple of modern *Othello* criticism without, as yet, any reference to the long history of silk production and embroidery in Cyprus that predates the play. Once *Othello* is repositioned as a Cypriot play, the conditions of silk production and embroidery become absolutely crucial to interpretation. These practices continued to form an everyday part of village life in the middle of the twentieth century and are still preserved today, practices that remain remarkably fresh in my mother's mind: the little village long lost seems as powerful now as a lifetime spent in the far glitzier West End world, steadfast, irrefutable, still weaving its magic despite the irrecoverable distance of time.

*

We used to buy the silkworm seeds from the village shop. They came in a matchbox, little black things, oval-shaped like sunflower seeds. You kept them warm for a few days then transferred them to a flat surface and covered them, keeping them warm still. What we did was, as they became small little worms we would feed them on white mulberry leaves, fine and tender and as they grew more we moved them on to thicker black mulberry leaves. Once they were big enough we moved them on to shelves of bamboo that your grandfather made. I used to feed them when they were on the bamboo – big things, six inches long with black eyes.

I was dead scared of them! I was a child, you know. Well. Once they were yellow we put small bushes, thyme usually, on the bamboo shelves, and they would hibernate in there in a peanut-like shell. When they were dried, we would collect them.

My mother and my grandmother put them in boiling water then and would pull the strands off the shell, pull them off with a spinning wheel or pull them gradually into a flaky ball of string spun round a spindle until it formed a thread. On the loom, what we used to call the 'voofer', we would weave the threads, long ways and sideways into material forming whatever pattern we wanted. You could make tablecloths, covers for church icons, clothes – your grandfather wore silk shirts all the time. Women would make their marriage trousseau – bed sheets, bed coverings and so on. You could dye the silk too, and most of the time it was dyed black for mourning. The bodies of the dead were wrapped in unwashed silk linen woven at home. We only had five mulberry trees, so we made things for our own use, but others would make silk materials, embroider them, and sell them. Materials were hard to find then, you know, not like now. These things were valuable to us.

*

These things were even more valuable in Shakespeare's day, valuable in a way that is difficult for us to appreciate in a world of industrialized mass production. Iago sets up the strawberry-decorated handkerchief dropped by Desdemona and found by his wife, Emilia, as proof of Cassio and Desdemona's affair, lying to Othello that with 'such a handkerchief [. . .] did I today I see Cassio wipe his beard' (3.3.440–2). When Desdemona admits that the handkerchief is missing, she adds that its absence alone was enough 'To put [Othello] to ill-thinking' (3.4.29). Karen Newman has pointed out that, in fifteenth-century Venice, possession of a woman's handkerchief was evidence of adultery, so its loss sets historically specific alarm bells ringing (1987: 155). As well as symbolizing excessive desire, Othello's 'first gift' to Desdemona (3.3.439) would have been understood as one of great material worth not to be given lightly; it was, after all, two silk handkerchiefs worth the considerable sum of twenty-two pounds that were deemed suitable as a gift to Elizabeth I from Sultan Murad III in 1593. These gifts were part of a diplomatic and mercantile exchange that saw Elizabeth issue the Levant Company's first charter for trade throughout the Ottoman Empire, including Cyprus, in 1581 (Epstein 1908: 16). It also saw the tentative exploration of military alliance in the face of a common Catholic enemy, Spain, an instance of how interaction with the Turk was as desired in economic or political realms as it was detested socially or religiously. Encoded into the handkerchief are the Anglo-Turkish anxieties that underpin *Othello* as well as the sexual mores of the *Serenissima*.

A very Cypriot history can also be found in the handkerchief. As far back as the twelfth century, silks from Cyprus or made in the Cypriot style had been bought by the English court (Monnas 1989: 196–9, 302; Jacoby 2014: 113), while 'cyprus' was the name given by Elizabethans to a diaphanous fabric of linen and silk (Mikhaila and Malcolm-Davies 2006: 37). In Paris, where fourteenth-century silk mercers often traded in England, 'Cyprus was best known for its high-prestige silk embroideries', especially those made with golden thread (Farmer 2014: 404–5, 412–13). The handkerchiefs received by Elizabeth I from the Sultan were 'wrought with massy gold asps' (Epstein 1908: 13–14n43), possibly made on the island or according to its traditions of silk embroidery. An endlessly complex and composite signifier, the handkerchief is also a cipher for centuries of material production in Cyprus and its consumption in Western Europe.[1]

The connection between the silk handkerchief and Cyprus was not only material but mythical. The early seventeenth century saw a flurry of instructional manuals on silkworms and the production of silk, including Olivier de Serres's *The perfect use of silk-wormes*, translated into English by Nicholas Geffe in 1607, and Jean-Baptiste Letellier's *Instructions for the increasing of mulberie trees, and the breeding of silke-wormes*, translated into English by William Stallenge in 1609. Preceding these was *The silkewormes, and their flies* from 1599, a mythic aetiology of silk in poetic form by Thomas Moffett. One of the narratives Moffett offers for the origin of silk conflates classical mythology with the pre-Fall innocence of Christianity as Venus rages against the fully clothed gods for her and Cupid's nakedness:

> *Revenge* she cri'de vnto the sire of *loue*,
> As she lay hid under th'Idalion tree:
> Affoord some raiment from the house aboue,
> If but to hide the shame of mine and mee.
>
> MOFFETT 1599: 5, original emphasis

The oath made from Idalion, now known as 'Dali' in modern Cyprus, comes to pass when Venus double-crosses Saturn. Venus makes Saturn lust for Philyra and Philyra for Cupid. Tormented, Saturn repents and promises the 'richest clothing for her Art | That now she did, or could desire in hart'. To keep her side of the bargain, Venus encourages Saturn to take Philyra in the form of a horse, a union that leads to the half-man, half-horse Chiron. Saturn then sends 'a Napkin full of little seeds', enmeshing the genesis of silk with Venus's overdetermined Eve. Mindful of the monstrous desires Venus facilitates, Moffett recants this particular aetiology because 'sith silk robes the blessed High-priest wore, | They were not sure the first fruits of a whore'. Yet, although Moffett dismisses the Cypriot beginnings of silk as too foul to countenance, their trace remains: comparing the tactile pleasure of silk to the thrill of touching another form of the scandalous goddess, he notes that a wise lover 'Delighteth more to touch *Astarte* slick | Than *Hecuba*' (Moffett 1599: 6, 7, 8, 74, original emphasis). In fantasy or in the royal courts, on the page or in the pockets of the elite, silk and silk embroidery had an association with Cyprus that was well established by the time *Othello* hit the stage.

With this association in mind, as an angry Othello lists the magical components of the handkerchief for Desdemona, the fabric of Cypriot identity then and now can be traced. Crossing and multiplying, these threads bring together the polyculturalism of the island that counterpoints the bitter bi-communalism of more recent times:

OTHELLO A sibyl that had numbered in the world
The sun to course two hundred compasses,
In her prophetic fury sewed the work;
The worms were hallowed that did breed the silk,
And it was dyed in mummy, which the skilful
Conserved of maidens' hearts.

(3.4.72–7)

The Greco-Roman communities of the island are invoked by the apocalyptic sybil, an ancient prophetess like the Oracle at Delphos who shames Leontes in *The Winter's Tale*. In the early modern period, these communities included the 'Grecians' Martinengo identifies as crucial players in the Venetian resistance to the Ottoman onslaught and which Avity counts as the most populous of the 'diuers nations' of Cyprus (Avity 1615: 1003), Greek-speakers destined to become the Rûm antagonists of modern ethnonationalistic division.[2] Above the Grecian peasantry sat the Latin Catholic elites of various monarchical families of Europe. As Knolles documented, these Latin Catholics fought long dynastic battles with each other and with upstart Orthodox rivals (Knolles 1603: 843–4), a royal mélange from which today's Latin Catholic community – as opposed to the Eastern Catholic Maronite community also mentioned by Avity – claim lineage. The silkworms echo Moffett's magical aetiology of silk that pitches Saturn against Venus, while the furious sewing of the sibyl once again brings to mind the needlework associated with the island and which Shakespeare preserves from Cinthio. Both the embroiderer and the prostitute in Cinthio are not identified as Italian like other characters, so we can assume that they are, like the composite Bianca into which Shakespeare morphs them, Cypriot. Cypriot identity in *Othello* and its hypertexts is in this way silently revealed.

This process of revealing what appears concealed provokes a broader question: at what point do we consider these literary figures – who come to Cyprus, who fight for Cyprus, who die in Cyprus – to be more Cypriot than anything else? In academic studies of Cyprus there is a growing trend that labels the Venetian, Ottoman and other stages of Cypriot history as 'periods' rather than 'occupations'. This emphasizes cultural variety over the notion of an Orthodox community dominated by a range of invaders and occupiers, and transforms these 'outsiders' into Cypriot protagonists. We could as easily assign the sewing to the Venetian and the Moorish or Islamic traditions of needlework rather than one exclusive to the island, but these are still not 'outside' influences: they are constitutive parts of everyday Cypriot life in Shakespeare's day and our own. *Othello*, many have argued, does not describe or picture its setting with the detail afforded more recognizable European sites. Quite the opposite holds. Specific political and cultural forces from across the Mediterranean are at work in the play, and these forces are the precondition for social existence in Cyprus.

This applies also to the mummy that dyes the white, strawberry-decorated handkerchief. It is white, isn't it? Many have long assumed it to be so. Recently, the tables have been turned on this staid idea that its red-spotted whiteness signifies Desdemona's stained chastity, a wedding sheet in miniature flecked by hymen blood that blasts Othello's eyes with a threatening visual reminder of his wife's all-too-real sexual body. Laying this myth to rest, Ian Smith has explained that mummy or bitumen was actually a commonly used black or brown dye that, in *Othello*, hints at the commercialization of black flesh fully realized by slavery (2014: 95–120). What constituted blackness and where it resided was up for debate in the sixteenth century: to be called 'black' or 'a Moor' could place you anywhere in Africa, Asia Minor or the Levant (see Barthelemy 1987: 7; Vitkus 1997: 160). But blackness in *Othello*, and the slavery at which it hints, cannot be treated independently from the Cypriot setting. Black slaves and free blacks are documented in Cyprus by the 1590s (Jennings 1987: 287), while the island has a longer intercultural history with Africa, and Egypt in particular, than with Venice or the Ottoman Empire. Cyprus paid tribute to Cairo's Mamluk Sultanate, who also weighed in militarily on the disputes of its elite. Malim's introductory history to Martinengo describes the island as 'subiecte vnto [...] the Souldan of Ægypt' (Martinengo 1572: sig. B2ʳ), while Knolles takes it to be common knowledge: '*That the kingdome of* CYPRVS *by auntient right belongeth vnto the kingdome of* AEGYPT, *you are not ignorant*' (Knolles 1603: 846, original emphasis). Christopher Marlowe opens *The Jew of Malta* with Barabas's account of the Mediterranean domains through which his merchant ships sail, with Cyprus counted as one of Egypt's 'bordering isles' (*The Jew of Malta*, 1.1.42). Links with the Arabian Peninsula stretch back even further to the early medieval Arab raids that pre-empted the Arab–Byzantine wars of Digenis. On the banks of Larnaca's salt lake sits the most famous monument of this heritage, the Hala Sultan Tekke, a mosque built in honour of Umm Harram, Muhammad's wet nurse, and one of Islam's holiest sites. Later, Elizabeth Lewis would describe the bulk of nineteenth-century Cypriots as a 'tall, dark, swarthy race'. Among them she encountered, at the darker end of the non-white spectrum, groups of emancipated Turkish slaves and an Ethiopian lineage referenced as far back as the writing of Herodotus (1894: 59, 230–1). Whether we imagine Othello to be a 'coal-black Negro', as G. K. Hunter awkwardly put it (1964: 51), or 'a Moor and therefore an "Arab"' (Ghazoul 1998: 1), Cyprus was, and remained, a fitting site for the darkness of both his skin and his handkerchief.

Further interactions and exchanges can be found in this silk-shrouded navel of the play. Many – Arden editor Honigmann included – have taken the Egyptian enchantress who Othello claims gave his mother the handkerchief to be from Egypt, rather than a Gypsy woman, due to accounts of women with magical powers in Leo Africanus's *A geographical historie of Africa*, which was translated into English by John Pory in 1600.

Africanus's descriptions, however, apply to the Moroccan city of Fez (1600: 148–51). The Egyptian backstory may provide a generic connection to North Africa, but the Elizabethan 'Egyptian' would become the term 'Gypsy': Britain's Romani people were then thought to trace their diaspora via Egypt or 'Little Egypt', likely to have been an appellation for a settlement in Modon, part of the Venetian Empire in the fifteenth century (Taylor 2014: 27). For Elizabethans, an Egyptian *was* a Gypsy. Could Shakespeare have deliberately given the nomadic handkerchief a suitably nomadic story? The Turkish-speaking Gypsy community of modern Cyprus is believed to date back to 1571, so a Gypsy enchantress would not have been anachronistic or misplaced there.[3] Slippage between the Egyptian and the Gypsy elsewhere invests stereotypical 'Gypsy-like' qualities in Cleopatra who, as Antony complains, 'Like a right gipsy hath at fast and loose | Beguiled me to the very heart of loss' (*AC*, 4.12.28–9).[4] The Egyptian–Gypsy crossover returns us in chiastic form to Cyprus: Antony makes Cleopatra 'Of lower Syria, Cyprus, Lydia, | Absolute queen' and Enobarbus describes her as 'O'erpicturing [...] Venus' (*AC*, 3.6.10–11, 2.2.210). Once more, we picture the goddess emerging from the sea onto Cypriot soil.

And where does the magical web take us next? Othello's contradictory imagery of virgin hearts literally pitch-black in their bituminous preservation captures in one line the play's deliberate tendency to present Desdemona as whore or holy virgin.[5] The 'Cypriot dalliance' that haunts the play returns: in the form of the stage imagery that connects virginal Desdemona to the birth of salacious Venus; in the form of the courtesan Bianca who also finds Cassio 'on the sea-bank' (4.1.133); in the form of the pre-marital orgies of virgin whores that linger at the edge of these events, an 'unhatched practice | Made demonstrable here in Cyprus' (3.4.142–3). That final image of maiden hearts turned black deconstructs the opposition between virgin and whore, between Desdemona and Bianca, between a marriage destroyed and another unfulfilled. Courtesan and embroiderer, Bianca serves as a literary trace of trades connected to the island in early modern material and mythical culture as well as a distorted reflection of Desdemona, who herself is 'so delicate with her needle' (4.1.184–5). When Cassio asks Bianca to put her embroidery skills to the test and copy the pattern of the handkerchief secretly planted on him, he delivers, intentionally or not, a silent promise of marriage. *Women would make their marriage trousseau.* With Othello watching from a distance, Cassio cruelly jokes with Iago about the prospect of marrying Bianca: 'She is persuaded I will marry her, out of her own love and flattery, not out of my promise' (4.1.128–30). Bianca angrily refuses to copy the embroidery. She suspects the gift for another, a gift she had every right to see as the precursor to something more, just as it proved between Othello and Desdemona. As both Bianca and Desdemona are at once betrayed by the same 'trifle', by a web of sexual intrigue woven in Cyprus, Bianca asks a question that could come from either of their mouths, one we continue to ask of Shakespeare: 'What did you mean by that same handkerchief you gave me even now?' (4.1.147–9).

*

The first time I visited the north of Cyprus to see my mother's village, to see the streets she walked to buy silkworm seeds, I committed an act that for some Greek Cypriots constituted betrayal. When the ban on crossing the Green Line was relaxed in 2003, many enthusiastically visited the homes, the villages and the friends they were forced to abandon in 1974. Filled with renewed hope for a solution, many showed their passports at the quasi-official border controls with the desire to meet, to mingle and to build bridges. Some were just curious to see what existed on the other side of no man's land; some just wanted to gamble in the casinos. Many others refused to visit the north. Anxious that this was not a political solution, refugee organizations suggested that no one should cross over until all those displaced by war were guaranteed the right to return. 'I will never go as long as I have to show my passport', was a common sentiment. An arguably more powerful psychical anxiety lurked behind the political one. The dream of return that fuels the existence of refugee organizations was slowly being eroded, as those who traversed the divide found homes in which others now lived, land that others now worked: 'Many people, when confronted with these realities, gradually began to accept that "real" return might not be possible' (Bryant 2010: 28). At the same time, a taboo was uncomfortably confronted: refugee return ceased to be an exclusively Greek Cypriot matter, as Turkish Cypriots travelled in the other direction to see the villages and old homes they too were forced to abandon. My family understood this before most. As I was about to cross one way, my sister-in-law was about to cross the other way. With her were relatives eager to meet her in-laws, in-laws who now doted on her. They were, like so many others, eager to see their old haunts in Limassol or once more to hang votive offerings on the tree of handkerchiefs, a terebinth tree in Paphos overhanging the catacombs of the Jewish or Christian martyr, Solomoni. Somewhat counterintuitively, when the Annan Plan was rejected the open border seemed to eventually cement rather than threaten the status quo of separated existence. Acceptance of this new, porous kind of separation came easily to Greek Cypriots used to partition and used to new, prosperous lives. Although Turkish Cypriots lagged behind economically and democratically, living conditions were on an upward trajectory. The continual and tyrannically pro-Turkish regime of Rauf Denktaş and the UBP (*Ulusal Birlik Partisi* – the National Unity Party) was also about to give way to the more open, more progressive Mehmet Ali Talat and the pro-reunification CTP (*Cumhuriyetçi Türk Partisi* – the Republican Turkish Party). Talat's appointment and the resurgent, post-Annan atmosphere of rapprochement it engendered now that people across the island could freely meet soon dissipated and, in 2010, the UBP was back in power. This time the hard-line Derviş Eroğlu was at the helm. Reunification needed a new vision, a new dream.

On the dead zone's edge I waited my turn at the Ledra Street checkpoint, a border crossing where an unpassable wall once stood. As a child I would stand on tip-toe and peer over the wall at nothing but deserted buildings manned occasionally by the odd, lonely soldier. Visitors to the old wall from around the world wrote the same message in the visitor's book over and again: 'Cyprus for the Cypriots'. I wondered then what this meant and I wondered again as I searched my pockets for my passport. Who were these 'Cypriots'? Was it 'us'? Was it 'them'? Was it the other Cypriots forgotten in the name of Greek and Turkish nationalism? Now the wall was gone and the full extension of Ledra Street was visible, Murder Mile restored to its full length via a small corridor of uneasy transition. 'Reunification' has become a complicated, equivocal term in a settlement process that, as a foundational and non-negotiable starting point, posits two separate constituencies governing ethnically homogeneous zones. A Cyprus of all faiths and tongues stitched together has almost completely fallen out of consideration, to be replaced by a solution that, if it ever arrives, will deliver a federal state of two dominant and distinct communities, warp and weft unwoven. I was about to enter a place no different from the parts of the island with which I was familiar and comfortable; it was a place still contested, its future still unresolved, its past still frequently and angrily rewritten. Many Greek Cypriots want to return, geographically and temporally, to a past in which they convince themselves life was peaceful until British divide-and-rule policies and American thirst for geopolitical power created the conditions for a Turkish invasion in 1974 to match the trauma of 1571. Many Turkish Cypriots see the same past as one that, if mimicked or recreated, will revive the exclusive persecution of them as a minority that dates back to 1571 and which the Turkish intervention of 1974 mercifully alleviated once and for all. Both narratives continually reinvent the past as one that makes the division of the island the other community's fault. One group wants the other to come as a visitor, the other wants to go as anything but. One pretends the past was a dream destroyed, the other that it was a nightmare ended. To cross the Green Line was not, for me, to see the village as it once was: I knew by now that I could never capture that lost past I longed to recover. To cross the Green Line was to reimagine, not relive, the past. To cross over was to reclaim the disavowed vision of the island as one of continual change, a diverse island in a region both 'multiple and mutable', as Iain Chambers said of everywhere in the Mediterranean except Cyprus (2008: 9). To cross over was to see the pan-handle landscape of my mother's childhood with my own eyes and envision Cyprus, and *Othello*, anew. To dream the island for myself. To find the magic in the web of it.

Act Four

OTHELLO You are welcome, sir, to Cyprus. Goats and monkeys!

(4.1.263)

Every summer of my childhood, on the anniversary of the 1974 war, my family would attend a march through the streets of London. Banners and flags were waved by old and young as thousands chanted slogans through Hyde Park, Oxford Street, Regent Street and Piccadilly Circus, or alternatively along the banks of the Thames – with Cleopatra's Needle over our shoulders – then past the Houses of Parliament and north through Whitehall. Whatever the route, the march always ended with a rally at Trafalgar Square where community leaders and sympathetic politicians addressed the crowds. Prominent in the crowd on these days was Mike, a large, hefty doorman with tree-trunk arms and a habit of bulldozing through police cordons. Mike was head honcho of the demonstration's rougher element. There was also beatboxing Little Nicky, tall and wiry, who, on account of his Spanish mother, suffered racial abuse as both a 'Dago' and a 'Bubble'. There was Big Nicky – so named to differentiate him from his jerky, younger cousin – an unhinged hothead susceptible to religious hallucinations and who, last I heard, was panning for gold in America. And there was tattooed Tony too, always laughing, always teasing, always pulling the glass eye out from his heavily scarred face and asking people to 'Keep an eye on that for me'. It was funny but never quite made sense because, really, wasn't he keeping an eye on you? On one occasion I attended a demonstration outside the Turkish embassy in Knightsbridge where this motley crew of streetfighters clashed with members of the Grey Wolves, a far-right pan-Turkish group who victimized and even killed journalists critical of the Denktaş regime in northern Cyprus and who attacked Turkish Cypriot supporters of the Annan Plan for reunification. One of the Grey Wolves' slogans was 'Cyprus is Turkish and will remain Turkish'. This was equal and opposite to the extreme Hellenism of Georkadjis, Grivas and EOKA, so I had to ask myself what kind of Cyprus Mike and his foot soldiers had in mind.

I took a closer look at what was around me on the next July march. The banners and flags all promoted Greek Cypriot village or refugee organizations. Everyone was Greek Cypriot. The bruisers I had befriended sported tattoos that merged the Greek flag with that of Cyprus. The chants were about the Turkish invasion, not the *coup d'état*.[1] Above all else – how did I miss it? – there was an absence. My brother was never there. This was not an event to which he could bring his Turkish Cypriot wife or their children. I realized then the deep-rooted nature of ethnonationalism: even when you wanted to demonstrate against the divisive status quo in Cyprus, you found yourself wrapped up, quite personally, in its politics of hate. Over time, my family withdrew from these marches and, while thousands marched through central London on those sunny July Sundays, we stayed at home. This retreat was our own political solution. The EOKA father chopping the salad fine enough to make it easy on his teeth; the mother reminiscing about the village she could not visit as she plucked or skinned the game; the grandchildren brought up to observe both Christian and Muslim traditions sniffing a piece of pork like jumpy teenagers about to smoke a first cigarette. If the political and military issues could not be solved, we had at least solved our domestic ones. On so many of those Sundays, when everyone had left or gone to bed, I turned again to *Othello*, for undergraduate essays, for my MA dissertation, for my doctoral thesis. One line kept catching me out: 'You are welcome, sir, to Cyprus. Goats and monkeys!' Where had I heard that before? Why did it seem so familiar to me? Didn't Mike used to shout something similar in Greek? Or was it 'Goats and cows'? Had he been misquoting *Othello*? Or something else? For whatever reason, the line looked strange on the page.

*

Othello studies have long seen this unusual outburst as the moment when Iago's smutty linguistic trickery irreversibly succeeds. This interpretation has become so entrenched that nearly fifty years ago Nigel Alexander considered it critical orthodoxy to read this as the point when Iago's 'images of bestiality and hatred' usurp Othello's 'terms of honour, trust and love' (1968: 74). Three years prior to Alexander's article, Caribbean poet Derek Walcott had deliberately overplayed the link between bestiality and blackness in his 1965 poem 'Goats and Monkeys', a cartoon satire of racism and stereotypes of sexual miscegenation. By the turn of the century, the phrase, which recalls Iago's perverse pornography of Cassio and Desdemona 'as prime as goats, as hot as monkeys' (3.3.406), had become an uncontested reference to 'bestial lasciviousness' (Doloff 2000: 82). But Othello's outburst has an afterlife more political than sexual. Cypriots, as Pilla writes, are more likely to ascribe it to the Greek poet George Seferis than Shakespeare (Pilla 2013: 365). Seferis first visited Cyprus in 1953, and in 1955 published a book of poems inspired by this sojourn, *Logbook III* or *Cyprus, Where It Was Ordained For Me*. One of the poems, 'Neophytus the Recluse Speaks', has thus far been omitted from major English translations of Seferis's work but includes the appropriation of Othello's words, an appropriation that has become one of the most quoted lines in modern Greek-language literature. And, recapitulated by Seferis as the words of a medieval Cypriot saint, Othello's outcry takes on a very different hue to the bestial sexuality assigned to it by generations of Shakespeare scholars.

'Neophytus the Recluse Speaks' begins with a quotation from the titular saint criticizing Richard I for the sale of Cyprus to the Knights Templar and mocks his failure to take Jerusalem from Saladin. Richard I's fleet was, as Knolles writes, 'by force of tempest there cast on shore' (1603: 843). The tempestuous waters in *Othello* seem, then, to be a nod to this widely known storm as well as the storms that forestalled Ottoman success. After this opening gambit against Richard I, Seferis's poem then pitches the futility and arrogance of the Third Crusade against the neglected plight of the island under its succession of Crusading medieval rulers, finishing with Othello's words: 'You are welcome, sir, to Cyprus. Goats and monkeys!' Seferis's historical critique also resonated with the times. Written during the last stages of British rule, 'Neophytus the Recluse Speaks' ties Richard I's neglect to the second-class status of Cyprus as a British colony, while the anger of Othello that punctuates the poem pre-empts the eruption of extremist and anti-colonial violence that coincided with its publication in 1955. Translating the English removes any sense of washing one's hands of Cyprus – *you are welcome to it* – an idiom the Greek words do not relay, consolidating the anti-colonial undercurrent. It also recasts Othello, who has the commission of governor taken away from him at this point in the play, as the deposed head of Cyprus speaking passionately on behalf of his people: Othello becomes a Cypriot saint and a Cypriot saint becomes Othello.

The medieval setting and its nostalgia for pre-Latin, Byzantine Cyprus suggests that Seferis saw the island as a Hellenic domain, but the power of its Shakespearean climax also shows that, long before I had started to see *Othello* as a play inseparable from the island and its socio-political concerns, others had done so too. And they did so in far more important contexts: a career diplomat for the Greek government, Seferis was involved in the Zurich-London Agreements of 1959 that established the constitution of the independent Republic of Cyprus. He personally aligned himself with the president-in-waiting of the new republic, Makarios, seeing the archbishop as a last bastion of pan-Hellenism in the

Middle East. Once more, textual practice had come to have a powerful influence on the lived reality of the Cyprus Problem.

So the Cyprus to which Othello spikily welcomes Lodovico was imagined by Seferis, just as it was by Mike and his gang of Levantine goodfellas, in a very specific way. Removed from *Othello* and inserted into the Byzantine nostalgia of 'Neophytus the Recluse Speaks', Shakespeare's line closes a poem that depicts a very different place to the one we see in *Othello*; it is a uniformly Hellenic space beset by one colonial raid after another, sidestepping any notion of the island as a hive of southern European and Greater Middle Eastern political and personal interactions. In *Othello*, these interactions reveal the porous, mutable nature of Southern Europe and the Greater Middle East. *Othello*'s Cyprus is fluid and polymorphic, constantly renegotiating the ideas of nation and nationality, ideas comparatively unfixed in the early modern period; the Cyprus of 'Neophytus the Recluse Speaks' is a closed site, originally and essentially Hellenic, enforcing the more defined parameters of twentieth-century nationalism. Seferis's poem thus comes dangerously close to repeating the historicizing contrick of Greek nationalism, which harks back to the Cyprus Wars and Byzantine heroism against the foes of Asia Minor in order to silently position Turkish Cypriots as belligerent outsiders who still refuse to go home. At the tip of Seferis's pen, 'Goats and monkeys!' does endure as a form of bestial abuse, this time aimed at Crusading – and, obliquely, modern colonial – overlords: it turns the tables on the dichotomy of a civilized Europe and its uncivilized opponents that was under construction in the early modern period and which was honed as a mode of exploitative production by Europe's mature colonial projects. But in the classic double-bind of anti-colonial resistance in Cyprus, it does so by subtly reproducing divisive nationalisms based on the imagined absolutes of an ethnic difference that cannot hold. Yet we might also read it otherwise. 'Neophytus the Recluse Speaks' disassembles the very Hellenism it assembles by finishing with the words of a man from 'here and everywhere' (1.1.135). Still Othello speaks. Still *Iago* speaks.

Progenitor of that infamous line, Iago, as much as Othello, emblematizes medieval and early modern Cyprus. Representations overlap in *Othello*. Venetians, known for their own internal diversity, are admired, yet also suspected. They are set against the spectre of the polymorphous Turks, feared and only begrudgingly admired, a gallimaufry of non-Europeans (and Islamized Europeans) who Henry Blount speculated in his *Voyage into the Levant* might represent 'an other kind of civilitie' (1636: 2). Blount's ambiguous comment posits an alternate, civilized culture and a culture outside the recognized, European bounds of civilization. The geopolitics of the Cyprus Wars animate this clash of civilizations, with Cyprus itself the prize at stake. That Othello, the 'extravagant and wheeling stranger' (1.1.134), embodies this encounter between East and West has become a cliché, if not one that ever extends to considerations of the play's setting. For Vaughan, as commanding an *Othello* scholar as exists, 'Cyprus's geographical and political position mirrors Othello's psychic situation' (1994: 22). The exploration of this fairly standard observation is, in fairly standard fashion in the field, eschewed by Vaughan. Does Iago not also mirror this 'geographical and political position'?

In the midst of describing the Cyprus Wars, Knolles gives a potted history of the island in *The generall historie of the Turkes*. Like Malim's introductory history to Martinengo's *The true report of all the successe of Famagosta*, Knolles's account revolves around King James II of Cyprus. This sly, murderous usurper cemented his place on the throne when he promised loyalty to the Egyptian sultan in return for military support against the Duke of Savoy. He then married 'Catherina the daughter of Marco Cornaro' (Martinengo 1572: sig. B2^v), an eminent Venetian, in order to solidify his position, a union that passed control of Cyprus to Venice after his death. Iago's name, and his destruction of Othello, may well point us towards Spain and St James the Moor Slayer, Santiago Matamoros, 'whom the Spaniards take for their patrone' (Knolles 1603: 663). But Iago's name also points us towards Cyprus's own betrayer of Moors, the one commonly known as James the Bastard. Shakespeare's betrayed Moor merges with Iago into James the Bastard, who, like Othello, married the daughter of a Venetian 'magnifico' and took her to Cyprus (Knolles 1603: 843). Latin amalgam, Turkish bogeyman, double-dealing bastard, Othello inverted; Iago manifests the assorted cultural, political and monarchical intrigues that moulded the Cyprus about which Shakespeare heard and read.

*

> He walks in to a taverna in central London with his brothers-in-law and there sits 'Thunder'.
> 'Thunder'?
> He only knew his codename.
> 'Thunder'.
> 'How dare you ghosts | Accuse the thunderer'.
> What?
> *Cymbeline.* Thunder-throwing Jove (*Cym.*, 5.4.94–5).
> I thought we were talking about *Othello*?
> We are.
> *Pointing at an empty glass.* You want a refill?
> In a minute. So there sits 'Thunder'. Eating. Smiling. Smiling and smiling. Like a villain.
> He lives in London now thanks to the colonial men. That's the deal. Passage to Britain in exchange for information about insurgents. And then the ex-EOKA man walks in. And . . .
> Well. I'm not sure I remember it right. I'm not sure *he* remembers it right. There's a red mist. First he wants to go home and get one of the Smith and Wesson rifles my grandfather keeps for hunting, has a rethink and goes back inside. Now either he calms down and insists they go someplace or *they* calm *him* down and take him someplace else.
> So that he doesn't do anything. At this point, why does he still care?
> I guess it doesn't go away, does it? People don't forget betrayals like that. Othello doesn't forget to kill Desdemona. For him the betrayal is severe.

So 'Thunder' is the smothered victim? The British were right all along!

Pour the drink, smartass.

He pours. I've been meaning to ask. Othello is a victim, right? Despite what he does to Desdemona. We're on his side, sort of, even now, these days, because we see where he's coming from, how he's been duped. We forgive him enough for him to still be a hero, right?

If we forgive Hamlet all the innocents he kills, directly and indirectly, then yeah, we do.

Othello is Othello, black governor of Cyprus. He's not forgiven as easily as Hamlet though, is he?

Course not. His actions will always be more criminal. His anger is 'unhinged', Hamlet's 'philosophical'.

He's governor of Cyprus?

Yes. Where you going with this?

Field Marshal Harding was governor of Cyprus too.

Ah, okay. I see.

It had to be asked.

Just because they're both governors doesn't make them equal. Harding's one of them. Othello is one of us, like Kurtz – more than Kurtz, coz Othello's always been more like us than them. What does the herald say? 'Heaven bless the isle of Cyprus and our noble general Othello!' (2.2.10–11).

The two are one and the same.

Yes. So maybe it's not even a matter of victimhood. On the inside and on the outside, Othello fights a Cypriot fight, forgivable or not, until death.

Unlike 'Thunder'.

It was late at night in a restaurant in the village of Dipkarpaz, or Rizokarpaso as it is known to Greek Cypriots, close to the rugged tip of the panhandle. A small enclave of Greek Cypriots has existed here since 1974. Earlier that day, I sat in the Greek Cypriot café, the only customer of a widowed old man as the busy throng of coffee drinkers in the Turkish Cypriot café opposite looked over in bemusement. Now, having walked through my mother's village and seen everyday life in the once-mysterious North with my own eyes, I leant on a friend to help me put together all the disparate pieces of the Cyprus Problem. The different, separate lived realities, as far as I could claim to understand them, on both sides of the Green Line. The contested pasts the diaspora relived and refashioned in the mini *zona mista* of North London, a faithful recreation and simultaneous radical reinvention of 'home' that probably constituted every word, thought and deed I claimed as uniquely my own. *Othello* was never far away from the conversation.

Trauma, from a psychoanalytic point of view, returns as repetition compulsion. According to Freud, when his grandson, Ernst, endlessly pushed a little cotton reel out of sight and then back into view again, the little boy's psyche was replaying the daily departure and return of his working mother in order to make sense of a distressing event beyond his control ([1920] 2001). But what happens when the trauma re-occurs or returns as itself? If my father's tendency to wake before dawn unconsciously manages the trauma of his pre-dawn arrests and 'interrogations' for the sake of psychic equilibrium, the encounter with 'Thunder' was different. When he first told me about this – a short recollection, a minute or two and then it was over – his anger was unequivocal. Even after all those years; even after he had left EOKA; even after the inter-communal violence of the 1960s; even after EOKA was re-established as the more extreme, less popular EOKA B in the early 1970s; even after the end point of partition in 1974; and even after his family had learned to live with and love those who were enemies throughout those three decades. That particular betrayal still ran deep. My father believes that his time in the detention camp was most likely the result of a tip-off by informants. He will never know for sure, but someone like 'Thunder' may have put him there. How was that information obtained? Was 'Thunder' also tortured in the dead of night? Was he too blinded by spotlights as bright as a ringside seat to creation's first, fiery blast? Did he capitulate to the pain where others had resisted? Or was there no definitive explanation that could rationalize his actions and help us manage their traumatic after-effects? Was he, in the end, just a double-dealing bastard like Iago or James II?

> It's like the end of the play. Othello wants to kill Iago but he can't get to him, can only wound him. Devils don't die.
>
> What about the women in the play? Doesn't Emilia betray Desdemona?
>
> But in that scenario both victim and perpetrator are innocent. Desdemona the victim. Emilia the perpetrator. Neither are villains to us. And I'm not sure she's a perpetrator, anyway. Yes, she keeps quiet about the handkerchief. But who says she doesn't snitch on Iago? In front of Iago, in front of Desdemona, in front of the whole audience, she says that 'some eternal villain | Some busy and insinuating rogue' must have tricked Othello (4.2.132–3). At this point she's probably saying about as much as she can – Iago tells her to shut up, even – so who's to say how that comes across on stage? Maybe she looks across, maybe she points, maybe she nods or winks or does something to show that she knows. And maybe Desdemona knows too. And knows there's nothing she can do about it too.
>
> That assumes that 'Thunder' has to be a villain. The information is beaten out of him, let's say. That information puts others in a cell.
>
> Or in a grave.
>
> But the victim and the perpetrator are both innocent again, like Emilia and Desdemona. You've got to ask yourself whether Emilia helps or hinders Desdemona and you've got to ask yourself whether you can decide one way or the other. So is 'Thunder' a villain like Iago or is he, like Emilia, a by-product of conflict forced into a position where everyone hates him? Not even the teacher likes a tell-tale. Who's the beast here?
>
> Who are the goats and monkeys?

Do people like him do what they do because those environments always pressure people into those decisions, decisions we can sit back and criticize?
Will you make that argument when you see the old man?
Yeah, sure. You think I'll make it to the end of the sentence before he sets the dog on me?
Don't fancy your chances.
Ideology can still tap you on the shoulder even when you turn your back on it.
Well.
Well. Shall we get the bill?

The owner brought the bill in a small velvet box. I looked across the table and asked my friend whether we had enough to pay for all the empty bottles. Both of them laughed at my gullibility as another bill was produced, a fraction of the price. The owner was a second-generation immigrant from Turkey, a child of the *Türkiyeliler* commonly held responsible for the increasing Turcocentrism of life north of the Green Line. He sat down, opened another bottle and nailed his colours firmly to the mast. 'My parents are Anatolian. They came here just after 1974. They are Turks. But I was born here. I am a Cypriot.' *Kipris' ta barış engellenemez. Η ειρήνη στην Κύπρο δεν θα εμποδιστεί.* Nobody can stop peace in Cyprus. Not even the 'Goats and monkeys'.

The strangeness on the page of that line still remains. Filtered through Seferis's poem, it becomes a vital political statement, one that points the finger of blame elsewhere – at Crusading colonizers, at the British, at the Islamic and Ottoman history it ominously excludes. Inadvertently, inevitably, it also points the finger of blame at the Hellenic ideal it formulates. That political afterlife serves a crucial purpose: it provides a firm, unbiased tap on the shoulder to a history of battling factions, a history of suspicions and betrayals. Finally, it points us back to Othello and Iago, both of whom can still be heard in 'Neophytus the Recluse Speaks'. And when they speak in that poem, they speak on behalf of Cyprus. They say 'I am a

Cypriot' with all the force that statement has come to acquire on an island where the violence – military, linguistic, literary – of unexorcized colonialist or nationalist ideologies targets the hybridity long conjured by those four simple words. In the search for a solution, even the federalist solution of a bi-zonal, bi-communal state of two distinct groups, it is those words that have compelled the need for reunification.

Act Five

OTHELLO   What noise is this? Not dead? not yet quite dead?

(5.2.85)

The first time I saw my father cry was in Cyprus. I woke up in the corner of the room that morning having rolled out of bed and cracked my head on the cool, hard floor. At the kitchen table he sat, cigarette in hand and in silent communion with the large windows of our summer apartment. My mother came into view, a mass of blonde curls and alabaster skin, and kissed my sore head better. The white surfaces of the interior shone with the morning sun, every revelatory detail of it and us ablaze in the humming dawn. How alien London always felt after a summer in Cyprus! How oblique, soft-edged and dimmed. He beckoned me over and told me that our trip to the beach was to be preceded by a visit to the cemetery where my paternal grandmother had been buried a year or so before. My only memory of this was seeing my father, bearded in mourning, walk through arrivals at Heathrow Airport after the funeral. Death's unspeakable magnitude was still beyond my emotional register.

By the Larnaca coast where the Ottomans first landed, we parked in a triangle of dusty gravel outside the cemetery's iron gate, rusted and locked. Whoever should have been on duty to unlock the gate, whoever should have been available to pass on a key, soon wished they had been. The bereaved have an irresistible authority to their anger. A swarm of spotted geckos and stellion lizards scattered suddenly from the path as we walked in. Pine needles crunched beneath my sandals. The cemetery was dry, bare, unkempt; ascetic in a way that might frazzle the brains of iconoclastic Protestant reformers obsessed with the satanic sensuality of Catholicism. Because this *was* a Catholic cemetery. The names were French, Italian, English, Franco-Arabic or, in the adjacent plot, Armenian. Some of the names of the dead seemed Hellenized, their provenance, if any name can truly have such a thing, lost in a swirl of migrations, translations and assimilations. The inscription on her gravestone read 'née Isseyegh', and before this simple yet totemic slab my father wept with great anguish, unreservedly and into his hands. Then, crouched down, his hands searched the dust, as if there he might find words more fitting to this final separation, a separation that trumped the geographical distance between them, which had never sat right with him anyway. When he was arrested for the final time, it was her room they turned upside down; when he was put in solitary confinement and beaten nightly, it was she, holding a change of clothes, who they turned away. My mother wept too, as if for her own. I was too young to shed tears for Anna; I even half expected an arm to be thrust through the earth for us to pull her body back to life. Yet I have become endlessly fascinated by her and by what her life in Cyprus might mean: a small piece of lost Catholic history. 'Née Isseyegh.'

The arrival of the Isseyeghs in Cyprus coincided with the journey made by Armenians fleeing the Hamidian Massacres carried out by the Ottomans in the late nineteenth century. Those refugees joined an already established Armenian community with a documented past in Cyprus as long as any other, a community that eventually included those who fled the genocide of 1915 to live peacefully alongside Turkish Cypriots. However, the name 'Isseyegh' does not end with a traditional Armenian suffix. Given the possibility of inter-marriage and names being changed or adapted, that does not definitively exclude Armenian heritage, but it is a big clue. My grandfather could not communicate with Anna's parents because they only spoke Arabic or French, so most probably they were from Lebanon, where the Maronites of Cyprus usually trace their medieval roots, or Syria. New to the island, the Isseyeghs were not part of the existing Cypriot Maronite community; this has its own, now largely unspoken, Cypriot Arabic language and its cultural home north of the Green Line in Kurmajit – Kormakitis to Greek Cypriots, Kormacit to Turkish Cypriots or Koruçam as it has been relabelled post-1974. Since there is no known presence in Cyprus, the Isseyeghs were almost certainly not Greek Melkite Catholics. The Lebanese origins still allow for an Armenian twist to the tale or the possibility that they were Latin Catholics new to the island, as opposed to members of the long-standing Latin Catholic rite. On balance, however, the likelihood is that the Isseyeghs were Maronites who emigrated from Lebanon at the turn of the twentieth century for economic reasons.

When Anna Isseyegh fell in love with a Greek Cypriot, the priest agreed to the marriage on the condition that the children were christened Orthodox. Still, it was on account of her Catholic heritage that Anna, estranged from her husband, moved her family from their small mountain village to Nicosia. They found a house on Kronos Street, just off one of the wide, tree-lined boulevards that guide you from the new city to the ancient centre, where these concrete tendrils of modernity finally wrap around old Nicosia's sandy Venetian walls. Within the Venetian gates pounded long ago by invading Ottomans, in the small old town's architectural palimpsest of successive colonial influences described by Bartholomaeus as the island's 'chiefe Citie' (1582: fol. 221^v), was Terra Santa, a school by Paphos Gate established in 1646 as a home for Latin Catholics during the Ottoman period. With a Catholic mother, my father could attend for free. From there he would take a place at a technical college over by Famagusta Gate, on the eastern side of old Nicosia and across the street from where Durrell was teaching at the Pancyprian Gymnasium. On days of nationalist celebration he would march through the streets waving the Greek flag. At the foot of the Venetian walls, on a dusty pitch, he would train with Olympiakos Nicosia, where the implementation of its constitutional provision to change kit colours from green and black to *enosis* blue felt imminent. Vocal in the streets and in the youth squad, my father was recruited to EOKA by Yiorghallas, the martyr in waiting. After the initial recruitment, he was sworn in as a member by none other than Archbishop Makarios in the Ayios Ioannis Cathedral, kissing his revered hand as the future president laid the holiest blessings on Cypriot Hellenism's latest conscript. When he was barely seventeen, when he had just broken into the first team at Olympiakos, it was on these streets that he threw his first grenade at British soldiers.

This particular story of Greek Orthodox destiny had an Arab Catholic beginning. Catholics in Cyprus are not visible in the way the more numerous Greek Cypriots and Turkish Cypriots are, their story often expelled to the outer reaches of the national narrative. But the Catholic protagonists of medieval and early modern Cyprus were as important, if not more important, than their Orthodox counterparts in Shakespeare's knowledge of the island, especially when he was writing Desdemona's death.

*

Both *The generall historie of the Turkes* by Knolles and Malim's introductory history to Martinengo's *The true report of all the successe of Famagosta* tell the story of Catherine Cornaro, the Catholic Queen of Cyprus and a prototype for Desdemona (Martinengo 1572: sig. B2^{r-v}; Knolles 1603: 844–5). 'Old money', Catherine was from one of Venice's most powerful noble families and married the Cypriot king, James II or James the Bastard, after he had secured his position on the throne with the help of the Egyptian sultan. James was the product of an affair between the Lusignan King John II and his mistress, the Orthodox Marrietta de Patras, who would have her nose cut off on the orders of the King's wife, Helena Paliologina, also

Orthodox. As a young man, James took up the Latin Catholic archbishopric of Nicosia, possibly manoeuvred into it by Paleologina in order to preserve succession to the throne for her daughter, Charlotte. Murderous and vengeful, James convinced the Egyptian sultan to support him in a civil war against his half-sister, her papal military support and the extra forces enlisted by her husband, Louis of Savoy, who was previously married to the Scottish princess, Annabella. James's successful move signalled the end of Lusignan dominance in Cyprus. Keen to solidify his position, he wed Catherine Cornaro, 'a goodly yonge gentilwoman' as William Thomas describes her in *The historie of Italie* (1549: fol. 109^r). James and Catherine were married by proxy and she, like Desdemona, left Venice to consummate her marriage in Cyprus. When both her new husband and, soon after, their newborn son died, Catherine would hand over control of the island to the *Serenissima*. Unlike Martinengo, for whom these deaths were unsuspicious, Knolles and also Contarini's *The commonwealth and gouernment of Venice* considered the king and his heir as potential victims of deliberate poisoning, assassinations that isolated Catherine and forced her abdication (Contarini 1599: 176–7). Knolles seems to suspect Catherine's uncle, Andreas Cornelius, who was slain by angry noblemen after the child's death.[1] Opinion turned against Catherine, and the Venetians, sensing an opportunity, intervened. Eventually, her brother, George, travelled to Cyprus and persuaded her to hand over the kingdom.

This backstory of ruthless cloak and dagger machinations reframes the closing scenes of *Othello*, with Iago outed as the mysterious and manipulative rogue assassin. Standing over the dead bodies of Othello and Desdemona, Lodovico pointedly addresses the malicious ensign: 'This is thy work. The object poisons sight, | Let it be hid' (5.2.364–5). The life of Catherine Cornaro also reframes Venetian geopolitical strategy. What Shakespeare read about in his groundwork for the play was Catholic and Orthodox elites struggling for supremacy; it was a power struggle in which Venetians were, as far as Knolles and Contarini were concerned, criminally involved and in which a Venetian teenager was an innocent victim. This backstory, like *Othello* itself, portends Ottoman invasion. Another multi-denominational prototype for Desdemona can be found in the aftermath of Ottoman invasion.

Geoffrey Fenton's *Certaine tragicall discourses* of 1567, a translation of Matteo Bandello's novellas, includes the story of an 'Albanoyse Capteine' (fols. 80^r–94^r), a likely template for Othello's emotional collapse. The Albanian captain falls in love and marries a beautiful woman from the Italian city of Mantua, then swiftly develops an all-consuming fear of his new wife's adultery because 'he thoughte every man that loked in her face, wente about to grafte hornes in his forehed'. Ovidian webs of entrapment return in the doomed wife's attempts to defend herself, attempts that 'spon the thread of her owne destruction' (Bandello 1567: fols. 86^r, 91^v). Such doomed efforts are made by Desdemona in her excruciating attempt to discuss Cassio instead of the lost handkerchief (3.4.32–99) and also her protestations of innocence in the brothel scene, as many call it. These protestations earn her nothing more from Othello than the title of 'strumpet' (4.2.83, 84).[2] The moral messages of Bandello's tale emerge in many other aspects of *Othello*. The tragic irony of Othello's murderous certainty about an affair manifestly uncertain takes its cue from the captain's irrationality: 'What greater signe or argument can a man geue of his own follie, then to beleue that to be true, which is but doutfull' (Bandello 1567: fol. 86^v). Emilia's tirade at the hypocrisy of men who are themselves to blame when 'wives do fall' (4.3.85–102 (86)) repeats the idea in Bandello's tale that some women justifiably 'enlarge their libertie that is abridged theim in doinge the thinge they are forbidden' (Bandello 1567: fol. 86^v). Behind this psycho-sexual morality sits an overlooked heritage of intertwined Catholicism and Orthodoxy.

The Albanian captain's wife is a Greek who fled Modona after an Ottoman invasion. Modona, the modern-day Peloponnesian city of Methoni, was known as Modon to the Venetians and contained the 'Little Egypt' settlement that led to slippage between the English terms 'Egyptian' and 'Gypsy'. Modon fell to the Ottomans in 1500. In order to marry this 'faire *Helene* of grece', the Albanian captain, himself from a country where Orthodox conversion to Catholicism has long marked deep-seated ethnic tensions, procures 'the rites and auncient ceremonies appoynted by order of holly churche [. . .] with all expedicion of tyme'. This seemingly innocent statement betrays the possibility that the captain's wife moves in the opposite direction to that taken by my grandmother and marries into, rather than out of, Catholicism. Or, alternatively, it suggests that the Albanian captain was converting to Catholicism because his wife had already done so for her first marriage. Or, even, that the captain was Orthodox, but converted to the Catholicism of his Italian employers to assuage fears about 'straungers' and the way they treat their wives (Bandello 1567: fols. 80^v, 85^v, 84^r). Every one of these scenarios could have a Gypsy start. We do not need to decide on or restrict the possibilities: their continual unfolding demonstrates that even when we step away from sources for *Othello* directly related to Cyprus, an interlaced, often peripatetic, Catholic and Orthodox history always returns. This entwined history has never been far from the surface in the south-easterly regions of Europe and the Mediterranean territories beyond.

Desdemona's death signals the end of this meshed Christian culture's dominance in Cyprus. A seventeenth-century London audience used to the ills and intrigues of Christian sectarianism, an audience all too aware of the ongoing Turkish threat to Europe, may well have spied an ominous geopolitical message in Desdemona's murder. When Othello – also a candidate for inter-sectarian as well as inter-faith conversion – smothers Desdemona, we see foretold the usurpation of a blended Christian elite by an emergent, as yet unseen, Islamic presence. The Greek root of her name, the 'ill-fated' Disdemona of Cinthio, hints at this doomed Greco-Latin mélange. 'Nobody, I myself', she says when Emilia asks who has killed her (5.2.124). 'Myself.' Who is that? An Italian who might be Greek, or, as

Catherine Cornaro would become, a Cypriot? A Catholic once Orthodox, like the refugee wife the Albanian captain slays in a frenzied attack? A Gypsy as nomadic as her Egyptian handkerchief? Née what, exactly? Née Isseyegh? Written into the literary and historical archetypes for Desdemona are all these past lives, their co-habitations, conflicts and hidden conversions. Each past life warns of Ottoman invasion and occupation concluded or to come. Desdemona's death recapitulates this warning, killed on ground soon to be trampled over by the Islamizing feet of invading Turks. The Cyprus Wars return, if they have ever been away, in the death of Desdemona, an event that symbolizes the transition from Christian to Islamic control, from the medieval framework of conflicts to the framework of conflict that has been dominant since 1571. As Othello suffocates Desdemona for imagined adultery, the Cyprus of ecumenist Christian elites gives way to the Cyprus we recognize today; it is an island dominated by the internal struggle anticipated by the Turcomania of Othello's subsequent suicide. Those same Cyprus Wars that reached so deep into the composition of *Othello* returned again in 1974, when Greco-Turkish antagonisms on the island reached their end point. Not yet quite dead, the Cyprus Wars of *Othello* cannot be separated from the war of 1974.

*

After the division of Nicosia in 1963, the Turkish Cypriots withdrew to enclaves and gave up government positions.[3] Anti-*enosis* feeling perpetuated by the nationalist propaganda of the Grey Wolves and the 'Cyprus is Turkish' movement morphed into the 'Turk to Turk' policy policed by the Turkish Cypriot paramilitaries, TMT. Turkish Cypriots were pressured into resigning from trade unions and those who had interaction, particularly commercial interaction, with Greek Cypriots were subject to heavy fines. Communist AKEL, the only party with members from all communities, was still haunted by a sense of betrayal for opposing EOKA during the emergency years and, in an act of political penance, gave their support to President

Makarios. For most, if not all, Turkish Cypriots, Makarios was an agent of Hellenism, just as he was for the poet Seferis, albeit from a very different perspective. Consequently, Turkish Cypriot trade unionists and party members were easy prey for TMT's enforcement of the 'Turk to Turk' policy. Willingly or under duress, those in the enclaves united in a Turcocentrism directed by Ankara that demanded partition or independent administrative authorities. The more factional Greek Cypriots were split between those committed, at least in the short term, to independence and others who still demanded *enosis*, even at the cost of partition. By the early 1970s, splitting the island between Greece and Turkey was the vogue solution. This 'double *enosis*' was facilitated by official Anglo-American diplomacy and covert American anti-communist operations in Athens and Ankara wary of any benefit to Russia from Makarios's non-aligned stance.[4] Only those loyal to Makarios rejected partition outright, and even they struggled to differentiate themselves from the *enosis* movement, including Makarios himself, who justified his resistance to 'double *enosis*' on the grounds that he wanted to one day give Cyprus to Greece 'undivided' (Drousiotis 2009: 73). Then a familiar presence from the past made itself felt once more.

In 1971, EOKA B (Beta) stepped into this polarized social and political environment, with Grivas once more at the helm and with backing from those loyal to the Greek military junta's shadowy strongman, Dimitrios Ioannides. Several attempts on Makarios's life were planned and attempted by Grivas supporters. One of these led to the murder of Grivas acolyte Georkadjis, probably for knowing too much about the failed assassination attempt in which he may well have been instrumental. As a response to a failed coup in 1972, a critical session of the Holy Synod aimed at ousting Makarios as archbishop was called by bishops sympathetic to EOKA B. When challenged on his role, Bishop Kyprianos of Kyrenia invoked the military campaigns in Macedonia at the start of the twentieth century: 'Long live Pavlos Melas. Long live Grivas' (quoted in Drousiotis 2009: 201). This reference to

Melas, a fallen hero of the scramble for Macedonian land, reveals the extent to which the Greco-Cypriot drive for *enosis* of the Athenian junta, EOKA B and their allies was inspired by the *meghali idea*, the irredentist ideal of uniting all Hellenic lands. The bishops tried to oust Makarios on the grounds that he held contradictory political and religious roles, but he resisted and subsequently retained the presidency unopposed in 1973. The day before his inevitable re-election, EOKA B bombed seventeen police stations. In a marked contrast to their original incarnation, EOKA B were now political outcasts whose violence was turned on those they had once claimed to liberate; Grivas was increasingly dictatorial and erratic.

Also in 1973, Rauf Denktaş replaced Fazıl Küçük as vice-president, a largely defunct governmental role that nevertheless made him leader and chief negotiator of the Turkish Cypriots. As the prime mover in the formation of TMT, Denktaş was a belligerent political representative for Turkish-sponsored paramilitaries in Cyprus. As EOKA B continued their bombing campaign against the state, bomb attacks became tit-for-tat between paramilitary groups too. Meanwhile, in Greece, a student protest at the Athens Polytechnic for greater democracy within the university system snowballed into a major anti-junta demonstration, one that precipitated the fall of military dictator George Papadopoulos. A second military coup was swiftly led by the EOKA B-supporting Ioannides, who came out of the shadows to put Phaedon Gizikis in place of Papadopoulos, a man Ioannides had long considered too liberal. A few months later, Bülent Ecevit, himself a strongman on the issue of Cyprus, was elected to lead a precarious coalition government in Turkey. Those Greco-Turkish negotiations for 'double *enosis*' driven by London and Washington were replaced by a stand-off. Everything was now in its right place to rip the island apart the hard way.

> *I took by th' throat the circumcised dog | And smote him – thus!*

(5.2.355–6)

ACT FIVE

With the same sentiment that the conflicted Othello, Turk and vanquisher of Turks, clocks out of his personal 'double *enosis*' nightmare, so the war of 1974 clocked in. 'Go for the jugular!' was the coded order from Athens for a spate of executions that preceded the *coup d'état* (Drousiotis 2009: 324). Grivas had died of heart failure in the January of that year, leaving EOKA B in a state of disarray, but the National Guard was still controlled by Greek officers under the direction of Ioannides in Athens. Tanks and armoured cars approached the presidential palace in Nicosia on the morning of 15 July, pummelling the building with machine gun fire. Makarios was inside meeting Egyptian schoolchildren. All major governmental and media institutions quickly fell, and by 9:45 am Makarios was declared dead. Later that day, EOKA veteran Nikos Sampson was sworn in as president by another of the anti-Makarios bishops, Gennadios of Paphos, and a puppet government controlled by Ioannides was quickly formed.

A guiltless death I die.
(5.2.122)

Orthodox folklore has Lazarus consecrated by Paul and Barnabas as the first Bishop of Kition, modern-day Larnaca, where he remained until his death. The Ayios Lazaros church was built in the ninth century around his second tomb. Desdemona's revival to restate her innocence offers a rare, perhaps unique, instance of on-stage resurrection in early modern theatre that echoes Lazarus.[5] Resurrection, or its impression, also happened in 1974. Paphos had not yet fallen, and an anti-coup radio station, Free Paphos Radio, was quickly set up. On the same evening of the coup, half a day after Makarios's death was announced to the nation, Free Paphos Radio broadcast his return to life: 'Greek Cypriots, you know this voice. I am Makarios. I am alive [. . .] The junta must not and will not succeed. From now on, the fight, above all else.' But the real fight was not to be against the junta.

Myself will straight aboard, and to the state | This heavy act with heavy heart relate.

(5.2.370–1)

Makarios was smuggled out of the country and addressed the United Nations Security Council in New York on 19 July. 'The coup by the Greek junta is an invasion,' he told them. Makarios's appeal for help was in vain: Ioannides invoked a litany of past battles with the Ottomans as he refused to offer diplomatic compromises while Turkey had already decided on an invasion, the 'Peace Operation' codenamed 'Attila' (Drousiotis 2009: 386–91).

Turkey had previously planned to invade in 1964 and 1967 by landing troops at Famagusta. Shakespeare never mentions Famagusta in *Othello* but scholarly consensus has always been that the port city must be the play's setting given its prominence in accounts of the Cyprus Wars. This well-documented prominence convinced the British that its ancient strength could be revived at the end of the nineteenth century, though the obstacles of disease and dredging proved insurmountable (Varnava 2009: 93–126). All these past lives were reanimated by Turkish ships that appeared off the Famagusta coast. However, as in *Othello*, these ships never reached the shore. The failure of the Turkish fleet in *Othello* indirectly suggests its opposite: the fleet, as members of Globe and Blackfriars audiences well knew, did eventually arrive to take Cyprus. Expectations were similarly confirmed and confounded in 1974 by the pre-planned invasion everyone expected would follow the long-awaited coup. The ships at Famagusta were decoys, and Turkish troops landed instead at Cape Kormakitis, by Kyrenia, on 20 July, five days after the coup. The scant resources of the National Guard were focused on protecting the coupists. After all the talk of the Byzantines, of a greater Greece and of resisting the Ottomans, the junta were now reluctant to engage in a war with NATO's largest army. *Enosis*; *meghali idea*; *long live Pavlos Melas*. When Greek push became Turkish shove, Cyprus was no longer considered Hellenic territory. Turkish troops met little meaningful resistance.

*

But whiles messengers run too and fro, the Turks violently brake in vpon them, and there slew them euery man. After the death of these noblemen the cruell enemie spared none: and hauing slaine such as they found abroad in the streets, brake into the houses, where they made hauocke of all things: yong babes were violently taken out of the armes of their mothers, virgins were shamefully rauished, and honest matrones before their husbands faces dispightfully abused, churches were spoyled, and all places filled with mourning and dead bodies.

KNOLLES 1603: 852

The description Knolles gives of the siege of Nicosia still makes uncomfortable reading today. *Othello*, along with its literary and historical sources, documents a time in which the template was set for future conflicts in Cyprus, and Knolles details atrocities that haunted Cyprus again in 1974. Systematic mass rape, including the gang rape of teenage girls, would lead the conservative Church of Cyprus to temporarily lift its ban on abortion. Thousands were massacred, their bodies dumped in mass graves. Turkish prisons became home to two thousand Greek Cypriot prisoners of war, most of whom never returned. Churches were destroyed and religious art looted on a massive scale. Neither were the atrocities in Cyprus one way. At Maratha, Santalaris, Aloda and Tochni, Turkish Cypriots were also massacred and buried in mass graves. Women and men, girls and boys, were dragged from their homes and raped. When the Greek military junta fell a few days after the invasion, a ceasefire was called and negotiations for a solution began. In violation of the ceasefire, Turkey proceeded with a second invasion, 'Attila II', on 14 August that would lead to it occupying over one-third of the island. Nine years later this area would be declared the Turkish Republic of Northern Cyprus.

Before I was born, in a small room over a shop in Bloomsbury, my parents listened to the events of 1974 on a radio. Chief among their concerns was Adonis, a reservist conscripted for the battle, who was missing. Fifteen years or so earlier, Adonis was collateral damage to another conflict. *They took one of my younger brothers into the yard outside, and as I sat in the living room I could hear them beating him up. Each time they hit him, I could hear him cry out. I was twenty by now, he was seventeen.* My father's brother now had his own fight. As the Turkish forces pushed southwards, the National Guard – a discordant medley of those loyal to the Greek officers and those loyal to Makarios, with a reservist supplement to boot – broke up. Heavily outnumbered, heavily outgunned and with no cover against the bombs of the Turkish air force, their few successes were, in the circumstances, remarkable and futile in almost equal measure. Presumed dead, Adonis made it to safe land beyond the line drawn by Turkish forces. He emerged from the orange groves of Koutrafas where he had taken cover, not yet quite dead, neither hit by Turkish gunfire nor fatally gored by a wild animal beneath the trees like Shakespeare's own Adonis.

The process of ethnic cleansing that accompanied the land grab of this second invasion made over 250,000 Cypriots refugees. Turkish Cypriots migrated to the northern territories under Turkish control and Greek Cypriots migrated to the south, beyond what is now the Green Line that cuts across the island and right through the heart of Nicosia, a city similarly besieged more than four centuries ago by the Ottomans Shakespeare read about in Knolles. The labyrinth of alleyways Bartholomaeus called Cyprus's most important city, alleyways in which the Ottomans rampaged in victorious slaughter, in which my father began a layered journey from Arab Catholicism to pan-Hellenism, all these winding lanes and too-narrow streets now stop abruptly at the barrenness of a no man's land that snakes through the middle to divide the capital, and the country, from itself. Where Knolles's description eerily prefigures the abuses of 1974, Othello's torn psyche prefigures the torn landscape of 1974. His final words echo through time, a metaphor for the violent artificial split of ethnic cleansing. The internal displacement within the self embodies the internal geographical displacement of Cypriots:

OTHELLO   Set you down this,
        And say besides that in Aleppo once,
        Where a malignant and a turbanned Turk
        Beat a Venetian and traduced the state,
        I took by th' throat the circumcised dog
        And smote him – thus!
                                                   (5.2.351–6)

This final fit of Turcomania articulates the psychological trauma caused by nascent concepts of nation and national self, concepts that in the modern era would harden and continually trouble Cyprus until the island and its people were rent asunder. Most emphatically at this point, Othello is a Cypriot through and through – in his polyculturalism, in his tragic attempt to eradicate it, in how he embodies the diversity he seeks to destroy. His condition is the condition of Cyprus. In Shakespeare's day, and more so now, both are refugees from themselves.

Uniting the factions at war over Cyprus, the suicide speech brings to a climax *Othello*'s repeated use of Cypriot themes: the brazen sexuality of Venus, goddess of an island 'where whoredome was openly permitted, and luxurie reputed commendable' (Avity 1615: 1002); actual and mythological silk production; the internecine Greco-Latin elites stealthily usurped by the Venetians; the Turco-Venetian Cyprus Wars with which the play begins and ends. Even the Aleppo setting of Othello's sacrificial 'service' hints at the common notion that the island was 'ioyned sometime with Syria' (Martinengo 1572: sig. B2^v). *Othello* acts as a nodal point for all these signifiers of migrant cultural multiplicity. Shakespeare's early modern vision was prescient too: this migrant cultural multiplicity has an ongoing afterlife – the Orthodox, the Catholic, the Muslim; the nomad, the Egyptian, the Gypsy; the Greek, the Turk, the Italian; the Armenian, the Lebanese, the Syrian. The Gordian Knot of tangled loyalties we see in Othello's last stand offers English literature's most resonant account of the Cyprus Problem, of the desire to separate these overlapping cultural threads at any cost. A desire that proved so costly to the island in the latter half of the twentieth century. If my love affair with *Othello* began with a desire to read it in the light of the Cyprus Problem, it ends with the conviction that to read it any other way after 1974 ignores a powerful political imperative.

*

We were not in a bar. A living room, sunlit. Glasses in our hands. The kids asleep in a toy-filled room.

The clock has stopped.
Again?
Again. But it's ticking, weirdly.
It never used to tick. Now it's bust it ticks all day.
A pause.
Wasn't there a watch?
A watch?
Yes, when Adonis was beaten up wasn't his watch smashed?
I'm not sure. I'll have to ask.
You know, I think you've left it out. The watch was smashed. Time was arrested. That moment was always with them, shared by them, after that. Or maybe I read it in a novel about Cyprus. I don't know. I might've conflated stories. Check it with your father.
Don't remember that. Maybe you *have* mixed it up with something else. It could be something I've forgotten, though. But, you know what, either way the idea works.
Time stopped for him. Up before dawn in the cells, up before dawn ever since. And for Adonis time stopped too, or maybe for him it was cyclical, came full circle.

So are we saying that time stopped or that it's cyclical?

Gesturing to the wall. Well, that clock will be right in half an hour or so . . .

Even a stopped watch . . .

Exactly. It was right in fifty-seven, fifty-eight, whenever it was, and it was right again in seventy-four.

The other day I heard someone talk about the 'monstrous generation'. They have no interest in the problem or its solution. They spend all day in cafés and bars.

Is that you?

I don't think that's what they meant. I hope not, anyway. But whether Adonis had a watch that was smashed or not, I think you're still right about time being arrested. All their lives these kids – I call them kids but we're talking about the post-74 generation, many of them are older than me – all their lives they're told to never forget the past. 'Γνωριζώ, δεν ξεχνώ και αγωνίζομαι.' 'I know, I do not forget and I struggle.' They learn this in school. And then all their lives they're told that there will be a future solution.

The clock has stopped for them too. There is no present.

Just a past that cannot be forgotten and a future that never arrives.

It's no different in all those sources we talk about, in the text itself. They all come full circle too. The past returns as the future. The future of 1974 was already written into the events of 1571.

Programmed. And yet, when it came, completely unpredictable. Foreseen and yet completely unforeseen at the same time.

Othello bridges the gap.

All the stories of *Othello*, like souls in the apocalyptic wall paintings Shakespeare knew so well, are resurrected by the Cyprus Problem. They shudder back to life like Desdemona. 'What's that noise?' Othello asks as his reanimated wife stirs. The trumpeting angels of Doom raising Anna Isseyegh from the dead to give her account. Raising Makarios from the dead to give his account. Raising Makis Yiorghallas from the dead to give his account. Raising Desdemona from the dead to give her account. The Cyprus Wars, Lazarus-like, fought again in 1974. Sounds echoing through time, like Othello's fateful journey: 'Come, let us to the castle.' *They put me in the van. I remember the words: 'Straight to the castle'.* All of it woven together. Like a web. Like a handkerchief. *You could dye the silk too, and most of the time it was dyed black for mourning.* 'And it was dyed in mummy, which the skilful | Conserved of maidens' hearts.'

Othello, a Cyprus play, bridges the gap.

'You are welcome, sir, to Cyprus. Goats and monkeys!'
'Καλώς μάς ήρθατε στην Κύπρο, αρχόντοι. Τράγοι και μαϊμούδες!'

The negotiations for a solution that began when the violated UN ceasefire was called in July of 1974 are those that continue today. All of this, not yet quite dead.

NOTES

Prologue

1 The terms 'Greek Cypriot' and 'Turkish Cypriot' are the standard descriptors, but we should think of the 'Greek' and 'Turkish' prefixes in inverted commas. This nomenclature has become an unchallenged norm, indicating the everyday linguistic tyranny of nationalisms imported from Athens and Ankara: Cypriots cannot talk about themselves without the need to define themselves as 'Greek' or 'Turkish'. That, prior to the twentieth century, Cypriots typically identified themselves as either Muslim or Christian, as people with different faiths but a common political identity, has been largely forgotten.

2 The term 'Greater Middle East' – coined by American political commentators at the start of the century and used by the George W. Bush administration to denote a homogeneous, unruly and predominantly Muslim threat to be negotiated by the West – opens the door for *Othello* to engage with other disputes, age-old or emergent, in this part of the world. *Othello* not only functions as a cipher for the abyssal complications of Cypriot identity but as one expression of a wider war. On one side are those who discipline, regulate or even exterminate difference by imposing absolute religious, national or ethnic doctrines and borders. On the other side are those who question those doctrines and borders, who exist outside them, who are violently penalized by their imposition.

3 References to all Shakespeare's works are to Arden's *Complete Works*.

4 This oversight also extends to performance. The Royal Shakespeare Company scheduled the two plays alongside each other as a Venetian double-header in 2015. However, the torture of detainees during the American-led occupation of Iraq was a

prominent theme in director Iqbal Khan's staging of *Othello*, an imaginative leap only made possible by the early modern Cypriot wars and given additional pertinence for us today by the frequent comparisons made between the abuses at Abu Ghraib prison and those in colonial Cyprus. This comparison was previously made in 2009 by Sadie Jones's popular novel, *Small Wars*, which followed the fortunes of an English officer haunted by tortures he witnessed in colonial Cyprus and which employed the Anglo-American rhetoric of the occupation of Iraq, such as the need to capture 'hearts and minds'.

5 A relatively recent disappointment in the long search for a solution to the Cyprus Problem has been the minimal impact of the Turkish Cypriot authority's decision in April 2003 to end a thirty-year ban and allow limited travel across the UN Buffer Zone – commonly known as the Green Line – that divides Cyprus. With a referendum on the United Nation's Annan Plan for reunification scheduled for 2004, the possibility of interaction and greater freedom of movement raised hopes for a solution. Despite resistance from the strong pro-Turkish elements in Turkish Cypriot political life, the Annan Plan was overwhelmingly accepted in the north, where living standards would undoubtedly have improved as a result of subsequent European Union membership. It was, however, rejected by the Greek Cypriots in the south, where the concessions required by the plan were perceived to favour the Turkish Cypriot authority and, by extension, Turkey. Much debate has ensued on how accurate or relevant that perception was, but the traction of that argument can, at least in part, be put down to the fact that many Cypriots on both sides of the Green Line had got used to living apart.

Act One

1 Makarios Drousiotis offers a brave, vital study of this understudied period in Cypriot history that sets out, in admirable detail, the dizzying array of proposals and rebuttals between President Makarios and Vice-President Fazil Küçük, both of whom negotiated on behalf of disparate, frequently factional, political and paramilitary entities (Drousiotis 2008, especially 21–56).

2 *Cyprus v Turkey* (App no 25781/94) ECHR 10 May 2001.
3 The Cyprus Problem has, for some, become a problem of property. Rebecca Bryant gives an excellent account of *Apostolides v Orams* (case C-420/07), as well as claims by Turkish Cypriots for land south of the Green Line in the Republic of Cyprus, and what all these cases tell us about the possibility for peaceful reunification (2010: 162–81).
4 Yiannis Papadakis provides an astute anthropological examination of the ways in which these two museums offer 'radically different constructions of the history of Cyprus' (1994: 400–19 (400–1)), a history densely packed between the two sites.
5 Anyone who has spent time with a Cypriot family will know that the only reasonable response to Desdemona's presence at the Saggitary, which we must assume is an inn or tavern, is to ask: 'Why is a teenager out so late at night? With a man? Of any kind? Why isn't she at home focusing on her education?'
6 The transition Shakespeare makes was not unusual. Venice was a common place of departure for European pilgrims and writers sailing east and continued to be so long after the sixteenth and seventeenth centuries. Henry Blount began his epic 1636 *Voyage into the Levant* from there and it was still a standard route when Lawrence Durrell made his way from Venice to Cyprus in the 1950s, a journey that spawned *Bitter Lemons of Cyprus*. Both in terms of the straightforward setting of *Othello* and its more nuanced conflicts of sex, race and religion, Venice can be seen as the stop-off point to Cyprus.

Act Two

1 Act 2 has often produced two key questions: Was the marriage branded unnatural actually consummated? And how long does everyone spend in Cyprus? The speed of the action belies the time they seem to have spent in and en route to the island. Have Desdemona and Othello had plenty of time to consummate the marriage or none at all? For some, this double-time crux, as it was christened by John Wilson in a series of articles for *Blackwood's Magazine* between 1849 and 1850, balances plot

development against plot structure, with any resultant loopholes not apparent in performance. For others, it was a straightforward issue of two separate stints of composition (Allen 1968). Most recently, Steve Sohmer ingeniously explained it as the clash between the Gregorian calendar used in Venice and the Julian calendar used in England and Cyprus, a Groundhog Day-style in-joke by Shakespeare (2002). Sohmer's fascinating analysis has its own double-time issue, in that the Venetians adopted the Gregorian calendar after the loss of Cyprus. Whatever the reason, the need to propel the plot alongside the time-consuming stay in Cyprus constantly points us to action off-stage. Consequently, at a time when both colonialism and racialism were in their modern infancy, *Othello* banishes the interracial couple, then continually interrupts the consummation of their marriage, repeatedly, obsessively pointing us in the direction of a sexual encounter it obfuscates.

2 In this sense, *Othello* and John Ford's *The Lover's Melancholy* are diametrically opposed in their use of the idea of Cyprus as a site of sexual transgression. Amethus – whose name seems to be a variant of Amathus, the ancient city at which, in *The Metamorphoses*, Venus prostituted her bloodthirsty nuns and turned their men into wild bullocks – makes this clear from the start: 'This little isle of Cyprus sure abounds | In greater wonders [. . .] Than any you have seen abroad' (*The Lover's Melancholy*, 1.1.86–8). From the barely concealed homosexual desire between Menaphon and Amethus, the cross-dressing Grilla, the story of Eroclea's abduction by her prospective father-in-law that echoes the pre-marital prostitution documented by Bartholomaeus, to Kalas's desire to lose her virginity and indulge in extra-marital sex, *The Lover's Melancholy* delivers on Amethus's promise, satisfying audience expectations of the lewd and lustful. *Othello* twists these expectations in the direction of tragedy.

3 On 30 July 2013, as part of a staggered release of thousands of colonial documents, Britain's Foreign and Commonwealth Office made public a previously unseen section of files on Cyprus from the emergency years. Some files held new documentary evidence of policies already commonly accepted, such as partition, but other files, although probably culled, were still of particular interest to veterans of the armed rebellion seeking compensation

Act Three: Part One

1 In its entirety, Varnava's (2009) *British Imperialism in Cyprus, 1878–1915: The Inconsequential Possession* offers a meticulous study of these first, frequently overlooked, years of British rule in Cyprus and documents the erroneous expectations of early colonial officials and the administrative changes that sowed the seeds for violent ethnonationalism.

2 This phrase has developed a popular culture afterlife, especially in cinema. In *The 300 Spartans* from 1962, for instance, Richard Egan delivers cinema's most quoted, and most heavily accented, line of Ancient Greek.

3 Turkish nationalism among Turkish Cypriots has, traditionally, been secular by comparison. This has changed slightly in recent years: as the mainland Turkish community has grown in the north of Cyprus, so has a more Islamic nationalism in line with the religious social conservatism of Turkey's Justice and Development Party, who have dominated the Turkish political landscape in the new century.

4 Communists were also targeted by EOKA and TMT (*Türk Mukavemet Teşkilatı* – Turkish Resistance Organization). In response to *enosis*, TMT supported *taksim*, the forced division of the island.

5 David French's (2015) *Fighting EOKA: The British Counter-Insurgency Campaign on Cyprus, 1955–59* is the first full study of the emergency years in the light of the Foreign and Commonwealth Office's 'migrated archive' at The National Archives.

6 M. M. Kaye's 1956 murder mystery *Death in Cyprus* was reprinted in the 1980s with an author's note that reflected on the division of the island since the novel had been first published. Kaye, a child of the British Raj and married to a military officer, bemoaned the 'greedy quarrelling factions' for the ruination of the idyll she once knew, glossing over the history of British involvement on the island ([1956] 1985: 'Author's Note').

Act Three: Part Two

1 Lefkara is a popular tourist stop for the lace embroidery said to have inspired medieval Venetian needlework. Village women sewing *lefkaritika* patterns on workshop steps have become picture-postcard clichés, but my favourite memory of Lefkara was the time my brother and I talked in the shade of some pine trees where old men were playing backgammon and watching the tourist buses – Russian, German, Scandinavian – drive in and out of a dusty car park across the cobbled road. 'Are you Costas, uncle?' I asked one of the old men. 'Yes. How did you know?' I gestured to a sign above his shoulder. Drawn on the wall behind him was a black arrow pointed at the faded canvas chair on which he sat. Scribbled next to the arrow were the words 'Costas relax space'. Everyone should have a relax space.

2 Thomas Kyd's *Soliman and Perseda*, a play on which *Othello* leans, functions similarly. A multifaceted Rhodes represents the last wall between Christian Europe and the Ottoman Empire, a battle fought through the prism of emergent Greco-Turkish antagonism, while the death of the Cypriot Prince symbolizes the fall of Cyprus in much the same way as Othello's suicide. The action of Kyd's play also turns on a lost token of love, in this case a necklace.

3 For more on Cyprus's Turkish-speaking and Greek-speaking Gypsies, see Marsh and Strand (2003).

4 See Mayall (2004) for an instructive history of the development of anti-Gypsyism in Britain.

5 The oppositions *Othello* constructs – and continually questions – between white and black, fair and foul, virgin and whore, are succinctly set out when the perturbed general asks, 'Was this fair paper, this most goodly book | Made to write "whore" upon?' (4.2.72–3).

Act Four

1 Greek Cypriot refugee organizations and lobby groups have explained the *coup d'état* as a short-lived pretext for the

unremitting brutality of the Turkish invasion. No doubt it was, but these groups also ignore the cultural conditions that made the coup possible. If Turkey's invasion was the ugly realization of *taksim*, a secessionist plan tacitly supported by Turkish Cypriot politicians, the coup that preceded it was the ugly realization of *enosis*, for which the 'Akritas' plan hatched by a cabal of Greek Cypriot politicians in the early 1960s laid the foundations (Drousiotis 2008: 106–9). Both ideologies resist any Cypriotization of Cyprus and insist on an unarguable ethnic difference between its 'Greeks' and 'Turks'.

Act Five

1 Knolles calls the Cornaro family the 'Cornelius' family.
2 In this scene, Othello also calls Desdemona 'that cunning whore of Venice | That married with Othello' (4.2.91–2), fusing the loose sexuality ascribed to Venetian society with the prostituting marriage cults of Cyprus.
3 In *Cyprus 1974: The Greek Coup and the Turkish Invasion*, Drousiotis (2009) offers one of the most comprehensive recent accounts of the events of 1974 and the antecedent years, and my account of events herein is indebted to the detail of his work.
4 Ian Craig and Brendan O'Malley's (1999) *The Cyprus Conspiracy* considers the key factor behind the events of 1974 to be Washington's longstanding anti-communist strategy in Europe, orchestrated at the time by Henry Kissinger.
5 Thanks to Lisa Hopkins for this suggestion.

BIBLIOGRAPHY

Africanus, L. (1600), *A geographical historie of Africa*, trans. J. Pory, London: George Bishop.
Agamben, G. (2005), *Remnants of Auschwitz: The Witness and the Archive*, trans. D. Heller-Roazen, New York: Zone Books.
Alexander, N. (1968), 'Thomas Rymer and "Othello"', *Shakespeare Survey*, 21: 67–78.
Allen. N. B. (1968), 'The Two Parts of "Othello"', *Shakespeare Survey*, 21: 13–29.
Allot, R. (ed.) (1600), *Englands Parnassus: or, the choysest flowers of our moderne poets*, London: for N. L[ing], C. B[urby] and T. H[ayes].
Avity, P. d' (1615), *The estates, empires, & principallities of the world*, trans. E. Grimstone, London: Adam Islip for Mathewe Lownes and John Bill.
Bandello, M. (1567), *Certaine tragicall discourses*, trans. G. Fenton, London: Thomas Marshe.
Barthelemy, A. C. (1987), *Black Face, Maligned Race: The Representation of Blacks in English Drama from Shakespeare to Southerne*, Baton Rouge, LA: Louisiana State University Press.
Bartholomaeus, A. (1582), *Batman vppon Bartholome, his booke De proprietatibus rerum*, trans. S. Batman, London: Thomas East.
Black, I. S. ([1961] 1963), *The High Bright Sun*, in *Mans' Book*, London: Odham's Press.
Blount, H. (1636), *A voyage into the Levant*, London: J[ohn] L[egat] for Andrew Crooke.
Botero, G. (1601), *The worlde, or an historicall description of the most famous kingdomes and common-weales therein*, trans. R. Johnson, London: Edmund Bollifant for John Jaggard.
Bradley, A. C. (1957), *Shakespearean Tragedy*, London: Macmillan.
Bryant, R. (2010), *The Past in Pieces: Belonging in the New Cyprus*, Philadelphia, PA: University of Pennsylvania Press.
Chambers, I. (2008), *Mediterranean Crossings: The Politics of an Interrupted Modernity*, Durham, NC: Duke University Press.

Christofides, R. M. (2010), 'The Politics of Language Use in Postcolonial Cyprus: Textual Seduction in the Mediterranean', *Interventions: The International Journal for Postcolonial Studies*, 12 (3): 415–27.

Constantinou, A. C. (2013), 'Cyprus and the Global Polemics of Sex Trade and Sex Trafficking: Colonial and Postcolonial Connections', *International Criminal Justice Review*, 23 (3): 280–94.

Contarini, G. (1599), *The commonwealth and gouernment of Venice*, trans. L. Lewkenor, London: John Windet for Edmund Mattes.

Craig, I. and B. O'Malley (1999), *The Cyprus Conspiracy: America, Espionage and the Turkish Invasion*, London: I. B. Taurus.

Dadabhoy, A. (2014), 'Two Faced: The Problem of Othello's Visage', in L. C. Orlin (ed.), *Othello: The State of Play*, The Arden Shakespeare, 121–47, London: Bloomsbury.

Dekker, T. (1600), *The pleasant comedie of old Fortunatus*, London: S. S[tafford] for William Aspley.

Derrida, J. (1988), *Limited Inc.*, Evanston, IL: Northwestern University Press.

Dessen, A. C. (1995), *Recovering Shakespeare's Theatrical Vocabulary*, Cambridge: Cambridge University Press.

Dixon, W. H. (1879), *British Cyprus*, London: Chapman & Hall.

Doloff, S. (2000), '"Well desir'd in Cyprus": *Othello* on the Isle of Venus', *Notes and Queries*, 47 (1): 81–2.

Drousiotis, M. (2008), *The First Partition: Cyprus 1963–1964*, trans. X. Andreou, Nicosia: Alfadi.

Drousiotis, M. (2009), *Cyprus 1974: The Greek Coup and the Turkish Invasion*, K. Pavlovich (ed.), Nicosia: Alfadi.

Durrell, L. ([1957] 2000), *Bitter Lemons of Cyprus*, London: Faber & Faber.

Epstein, M. (1908), *The Early History of the Levant Company*, London: George Routledge.

Farmer, S. (2014), 'Medieval Paris and the Mediterranean: The Evidence from the Silk Industry', *French Historical Studies*, 37 (3): 383–419.

Ford, J. (1995), *The Lover's Melancholy*, in *'Tis Pity She's a Whore and Other Plays*, M. Lomax (ed.), Oxford: Oxford University Press.

French, D. (2015), *Fighting EOKA: The British Counter-Insurgency Campaign on Cyprus, 1955–59*, Oxford: Oxford University Press.

Freud, S. ([1920] 2001), 'Beyond the Pleasure Principle', in
J. Strachey, A. Freud, A. Strachey and A. Tyson (eds.), *The Standard Edition of The Complete Psychological Works of Sigmund Freud, Vol. XVIII (1920–1922): Beyond the Pleasure Principal, Group Psychology and Other Works (1920–1922)*, 3–66, London: Vintage.

Gentleman, F. (1770), *The Dramatic Censor; Or, Critical Companion. Volume the First*, London: J. Bell and C. Etherington.

Ghazoul, F. J. (1998), 'The Arabization of *Othello*', *Comparative Literature*, 50 (1): 1–31.

Given, M. (2002), 'Corrupting Aphrodite: Colonialist Interpretations of the Cyprian Goddess', in D. Bolger and N. Serwint (eds.), *Engendering Aphrodite: Women and Society in Ancient Cyprus*, 419–28, Boston, MA: American Schools of Oriental Research.

Greene, R. (1585), *Planetomachia: or the first parte of the generall opposition of the seuen planets*, London: [T. Dawson and G. Robinson] for T. Cadman.

Hibbard, G. (1968), '"Othello" and the Pattern of Shakespearean Tragedy', *Shakespeare Survey*, 21: 39–46.

Honigmann, E. A. J. (ed.) ([1997] 2014), *Othello*, The Arden Shakespeare, London: Bloomsbury.

Hunter, G. K. (1964), 'Elizabethans and Foreigners', *Shakespeare Survey*, 17: 37–52.

Jacoby, D. (2014), 'Cypriot Gold Thread in Late Medieval Silk Weaving and Embroidery', in S. B. Edgington and H. J. Nicholson (eds.), *Deeds Done Beyond the Sea: Essays on William of Tyre, Cyprus and the Military Orders Presented to Peter Edbury*, 101–14, Farnham, UK: Ashgate.

Jennings, R. C. (1987), 'Black Slaves and Free Blacks in Ottoman Cyprus, 1590–1640', *Journal of the Economic and Social History of the Orient*, 30 (3): 286–302.

Jones, E. (1968), '"Othello", "Lepanto" and the Cyprus Wars', *Shakespeare Survey*, 21: 47–52.

Jones, S. (2009), *Small Wars*, London: Chatto & Windus.

Kaye, M. M. ([1956] 1985), *Death in Cyprus*, London: Penguin.

Keller, S. D. (2010), 'Combining Rhetoric and Pragmatics to Read *Othello*', *English Studies*, 91 (4): 398–411.

Knolles, R. (1603), *The generall historie of the Turkes*, London: Adam Islip.

Levith, M. J. (1989), *Shakespeare's Italian Settings and Plays*, Basingstoke, UK: Macmillan.
Lewis, E. A. M. (1894), *A Lady's Impression of Cyprus in 1893*, London: Remington.
Loomba, A. (1989), *Gender, Race, Renaissance Drama*, Manchester: Manchester University Press.
Loomba, A. (2002), *Shakespeare, Race, and Colonialism*, Oxford: Oxford University Press.
Mallin, E. S. (2012), 'Othello, Marriage, Middle Age', in W. McKenzie and T. Papadopoulou (eds.), *Shakespeare and I*, Shakespeare Now!, 40–60, London: Continuum.
Marlowe, C. (1997), *The Jew of Malta*, D. Bevington (ed.), Revels Student Editions, Manchester: Manchester University Press.
Marsh, A. and E. Strand (2003), '". . . spies, deserters and undesirable persons. . . .": The Gypsies of Cyprus, 1322–2003', *KURI: Journal of the Dom Research Centre*, 1 (8). Available online: http://www.domresearchcenter.com/journal/18/cyprus8.html (accessed 25 May 2015).
Marston, J. (1598a), *The metamorphosis of Pigmalions image*, London: Edmond Matts.
Marston, J. (1598b), *The scourge of villanie. Three bookes of satyres*, London: J[ames] R[oberts].
Martinengo, C. N. (1572), *The true report of all the successe of Famagosta*, trans. W. Malim, London: John Daye.
Mayall, D. (2004), *Gypsy Identities, 1500–2000: From Egipcyans and Moon-men to the Ethnic Romany*, London: Routledge.
Mendonça, B. H. C. de, (1968), '"Othello": A Tragedy Built on Comic Structure', *Shakespeare Survey*, 21: 31–8.
Mikhaila, N. and J. Malcolm-Davies (2006), *The Tudor Tailor: Reconstructing Sixteenth-Century Dress*, London: Batsford.
Mirabella, B. (2011), '"A Wording Poet": Othello Among the Mountebanks', *Medieval & Renaissance Drama in England*, 24: 150–75.
Moffett, T. (1599), *The silkewormes, and their flies*, London: V[alentine] S[imms] for Nicholas Ling.
Moisan, T. (1991), 'Repetition and Interrogation in Othello: "What needs this iterance?" or, "Can anything be made of this?"', in V. M. Vaughan and K. Cartwright (eds.), *Othello: New Perspectives*, 48–73, Rutherford, NJ: Fairleigh Dickinson University Press/London: Associated University Presses.

Monnas, L. (1989), 'Silk Cloths Purchased for the Great Wardrobe of the Kings of England, 1325–1462', *Textile History*, 20 (2): 283–307.

Neill, M. (1989), 'Unproper Beds: Race, Adultery, and the Hideous in *Othello*', *Shakespeare Quarterly*, 40 (4): 383–412.

Neill, M. (1998), '"Mulattos", "Blacks", and "Indian Moors": *Othello* and Early Modern Constructions of Human Difference', *Shakespeare Quarterly*, 49 (4): 261–74.

Newman, K. (1987), '"And wash the Ethiop White": Femininity and the Monstrous in *Othello*', in J. E. Howard and M. F. O'Connor (eds.), *Shakespeare Reproduced: The Text in History and Ideology*, 143–62, London: Methuen.

Orlin, L. C. (ed.), (2014), *Othello: The State of Play*, The Arden Shakespeare, London: Bloomsbury.

Ovid (1567), *The. xv. bookes of P. Ouidius Naso, entytuled Metamorphosis*, trans. A. Golding, London: William Seres.

Papadakis, Y. (1994), 'The National Struggle Museums of a Divided City', *Ethnic and Racial Studies*, 17 (3): 400–19.

Papadakis, Y. (2005), *Echoes from the Dead Zone: Across the Cyprus Divide*, London: I. B. Taurus.

Papadakis, Y. (2006), 'Aphrodite Delights', *Postcolonial Studies*, 9 (3): 237–50.

Papapavlou, A. N. (1998), 'Attitudes toward the Greek Cypriot Dialect: Sociocultural Implications', *International Journal of the Sociology of Language*, 134: 15–28.

Pilla, E. (2013), 'Review of Shakespeare's *Othello* (directed by Nikos Charalambous for the Cyprus Theatre Organization) at the Latsia Municipal Theatre, Nicosia, Cyprus, 27 November 2010', *Shakespeare*, 9 (3): 365–6.

Ronk, M. (2005), 'Desdemona's Self-Presentation', *English Literary Renaissance*, 35 (1): 52–72.

Rymer, T. (1693), *A short view of tragedy*, London: Richard Baldwin.

Scragg, L. (1968), 'Iago – Vice or Devil?', *Shakespeare Survey*, 21: 53–65.

Seferis, G. (1955), 'Νεόφυτος ο εγκλειστος μιλά –' (Neophytus the Recluse Speaks). Available online: http://www.greek-language.gr/Resources/literature/tools/concordance/browse.html?cnd_id=1&text_id=1672 (accessed 25 May 2015).

Shakespeare, W. (2011), *The Arden Shakespeare Complete Works*, R. Proudfoot, A. Thompson and D. S. Kastan (eds.), London: Bloomsbury.

Smith, I. (2014), 'Othello's Black Handkerchief', in L. C. Orlin (ed.), *Othello: The State of Play*, The Arden Shakespeare, 95–120, London: Bloomsbury.

Sohmer, S. (2002), 'The "Double Time" Crux in *Othello* Solved', *English Literary Renaissance*, 32 (2): 214–38.

Spivack, B. (1958), *Shakespeare and the Allegory of Evil: The History of a Metaphor in Relation to his Major Villains*, New York: Columbia University Press.

Taylor, B. (2014), *Another Darkness, Another Dawn: A History of Gypsies, Roma and Travellers*, London: Reaktion.

Theobald, L. (1733), *The Works of Shakespeare*, vol. 6, London: A. Bettesworth, C. Hitch, J. Tonson, F. Clay, W. Feales and R. Wellington.

Thomas, W. (1549), *The historie of Italie*, London: Thomas Berthelet.

Tosi, L. and S. Bassi (eds.), (2011), *Visions of Venice in Shakespeare*, Farnham, UK: Ashgate.

Varnava, A. (2009), *British Imperialism in Cyprus, 1878–1915: The Inconsequential Possession*, Manchester: Manchester University Press.

Vaughan, V. M. (1994), *Othello: A Contextual History*, Cambridge: Cambridge University Press.

Vaughan, V. M. (2011), 'Supersubtle Venetians: Richard Knolles and the Geopolitics of Shakespeare's *Othello*', in L. Tosi and S. Bassi (eds.), *Visions of Venice in Shakespeare*, 19–32, Farnham, UK: Ashgate.

Vitkus, D. J. (1997), 'Turning Turk in *Othello*: The Conversion and Damnation of the Moor', *Shakespeare Quarterly*, 48 (2): 145–76.

Vitkus, D. J. (ed.), (2000), *Three Turk Plays from Early Modern England: Selimus, A Christian Turned Turk, and The Renegado*, New York: Columbia University Press.

Walcott, D. (1965), 'Goats and Monkeys', *The Castaway*, London: Jonathan Cape.

Walsh, M. J. K. (2012), 'Othello, "Turn[ing] Turks" and Cornelis de Bruyn's Copperplate of the Ottoman Port of Famagusta in the Seventeenth Century', *The Mariner's Mirror*, 98 (4): 448–66.

Weimann, R. and D. Bruster (2008), *Shakespeare and the Power of Performance: Stage and Page in the Elizabethan Theatre*, Cambridge: Cambridge University Press.

Wells, S. (2011), 'Foreword', in L. Tosi and S. Bassi (eds.), *Visions of Venice in Shakespeare*, Farnham, UK: Ashgate.

INDEX

Africanus, Leo, *A geographical historie of Africa*, 66–7
Afxentiou, Grigoris, 46–7
Agamben, Georgio, 53–4
AKEL, 92–3. *See also* EOKA: and communists
Akıncı, Mustafa, 16
Alexander, Nigel, 75
Allot, Robert, *England's Parnassus*,
    John Harrington's 'Of Cyprus' in, 32
    Venus poem by 'D. Lodge' in, 34
Amathus, 30, 106n2. *See also* Ford, John; Ovid
America,
    and the Greater Middle East, 103n2
    and Iraq War, 103–4n4
    and 1974 war, 70, 93, 94, 109n4
Annan Plan for Cyprus, 20, 69, 74, 104n5
Antony and Cleopatra, 34, 36, 67
Apostolides v Orams, 19, 105n3
Arab-Byzantine wars, 46, 66
Armenians, 86–7
Atatürk, Mustafa Kemal, 9, 11
Avity, Pierre d', *The estates, empires, & principallities of the world*,
    prostituting cults of Cyprus in, 43–4, 99
    Cypriot demography in, 64

Bandello, Matteo, *Certaine tragicall discourses*, 90–2
Bartholomaeus, *De Proprietatibus Rerum*
    prostituting cults of Cyprus in, 29–30, 38, 106n2
    Nicosia in, 87, 98
Batman, Stephen. *See* Bartholomaeus
Battle of Lepanto, 18
Black, Ian Stuart, *The High Bright Sun*, 56
blackness, 65–6
Blair, Cherie, 19
Blount, Henry, *Voyage into the Levant*, 78, 105n6
Botero, Giovanni, *The worlde*, 27–8
Bradley, A. C., 37
Bragadin, Marco Antonio, 29
British colonial rule, 9
    and colonialist literature. *See* Black, Ian Stuart; Dixon, William Hepworth; Durrell, Lawrence; Kaye, M. M.; Lewis, Elizabeth
    Cypriot war-time volunteers during, 59
    early period, 45–6

emergency years. *See* EOKA: detention and torture of suspected members of; ideology and formation
divide and rule policies of, 11, 41, 70
torture during. *See* EOKA: detention and torture of suspected members of
and Shakespeare studies, 6, 13–15
and 1974 war (post-colonial influence), 10, 20, 93
See also Famagusta: British attempts to revive; sexuality: during British rule; Vice (medieval allegory): in relation to British colonial interrogations
Bruyn, Cornelis de, 13
Bryant, Rebecca, 69, 105n3,

Camp 'K' detention centre (Kokkinotrimithia), 2, 48–9, 51–3
Catholics (Latin), 64, 86–8
in relation to *Othello*, 88–92
Chambers, Iain, 71
Christofias, Dimitris, 52. *See also* AKEL.
Christofides, Adonis, 98, 100–1
Cinthio, *Hecatommithi*, 8, 17, 31, 64, 91
Constantinou, Angelo C., 38, 39
Contarini, Gasper, *The commonwealth and gouernment of Venice*, 27–8, 89–90
conversion, 11–14, 25, 28, 91–2

Cornaro, Catherine, Queen of Cyprus, 12, 78, 88–90, 92
Crusaders, 45, 76–7, 83
Cupid, 37, 63
Cymbeline, 35, 36–7, 79
Cyprus Wars,
and *Othello*, 7–8, 17–18, 29, 46–7, 78, 92, 96, 99
in modern Cyprus, 20–1, 77, 102
and Shakespeare studies, 5–6, 12–15
See also Battle of Lepanto; Cinthio; EOKA: ideology and formation; Knolles, Richard; Martinengo, Conte Nestore

Daborne, Richard, *A Christian Turn'd Turk*, 28
Dadabhoy, Ambereen, 13
Dekker, Thomas, *Old Fortunatus*, 32
Denktaş, Rauf, 69, 74, 94
Derrida, Jacques, 2
Dessen, Alan C., 33
Devil (medieval allegory). *See* Vice
double-time crux, 105–6n1
Digenis Akritas. *See* Arab-Byzantine wars of Cyprus
Dipkarpaz (Rizokarpaso), 80–1
Dixon, William Hepworth, 40–1, 45
Doloff, Steven, 34–5, 75
Drousiotis, Makarios,
on 1974 war, 93, 95, 96, 108–9n1, 109n3
on 1960s inter-communal strife, 21, 104n1

Dudley, Robert, Earl of Leicester, 29
Durrell, Lawrence
 teaching 21, 87
 Bitter Lemons of Cyprus, 56, 105n6

Ecevit, Bülent, 94
Egypt,
 Cyprus and, 66, 78, 88–9, 100
 enchantress in *Othello* from, 66–7,
 schoolchildren in 1974 war from, 95
 slippage between 'Gypsy' and, 67, 90–1, 92
Elizabeth I, 29, 62
enosis. See EOKA, especially 'ideology and formation'; EOKA B; *taksim*
EOKA
 and Shakespeare studies, 14
 ideology and formation, 5, 39–40, 46–7
 detention and torture of suspected members of, 5, 47–50, 55–7, 79–83, 103–4 n4, 106n3, 107n5
 and communists, 47, 92–3, 107n4
 recruitment, 88
 veteran Nikos Sampson, 95. *See also* EOKA B.
 veteran Tassos Papadopoulos, 19
 veteran Polycarpos Georkadjis, 21, 74, 93
EOKA B, 81, 93–5
Eroğlu, Derviş, 69

ethnic cleansing, 8, 10, 21, 98–9
 in relation to *Othello*, 8, 98–9

Famagusta
 British attempts to revive, 96
 citadel. *See* Othello's Tower.
 early modern depictions of, 10–11, 13, 32
 as setting of *Othello*, 96
 Ottoman conquest of, 29
 planned Turkish invasions of, 96
Fenton, Geoffrey. *See* Bandello, Matteo.
Ford, John, *The Lover's Melancholy*, 10, 106n2
Free Paphos Radio, 95
Freud, Sigmund, 81

Gentleman, Francis, 12–13
Greek military junta, 10, 93–7
Greek nationalism. *See* nationalism
Greene, Robert, 34
Grey Wolves, 74, 92
Grivas, Georgios,
 as EOKA leader, 46–7, 74
 as EOKA B leader, 93–5
Gypsies, 66–7, 90–1, 92

Hamlet, 80
handkerchiefs. *See* Paphos: Tree of Handkerchiefs; silk production
Harding, Sir John, 47, 55, 80
Hermaphroditus, 41
Honigmann, E. A. J., 31, 66
Hunter, G. K., 66

Ioannides, Dimitrios. *See* Greek military junta
Isseyegh, Anna, 85–8, 92, 101

James I, *The Lepanto*, 17–18
James II of Cyprus, 12, 78–9, 82, 88–9
Jones, Emrys, 14

Kaye, M. M., *Death in Cyprus*, 107n6
Keller, Stefan D., 52
Key club (Acropole Hotel), 39, 50. *See also* Nicosia: cabaret industry
Knolles, Richard, *The generall historie of the Turkes*,
    Cypriot demography in, 64
    Cypriot history in, 12, 66, 76, 78–9, 88–90
    Cyprus Wars and siege of Nicosia in, 13, 29, 97–9
    St James the Moor Slayer in, 78. *See also* St James the Moor Slayer.
Küçük, Fazil, 94, 104n1
Kyd, Thomas, *Soliman and Perseda*, 108n2
Kyrenia,
    Bishop Kyprianos of, 93
    Castle prison, 2, 48
    in the 1974 war, 96

Larnaca, 8, 51
    consecration of Lazarus in, 95
    Hala Sultan Tekke, 66
    Ottoman invasion of, 85
Ledra Palace Hotel, 21–2
Ledra Street, 21–2, 39, 69–71

Levant Company, 15, 62
Levith, Murray J., 14
Lewis, Elizabeth, *A Lady's Impression of Cyprus in 1893*, 40–1, 45, 66
Lewkenor, Lewes. *See* Contarini, Gasper
London (Cypriot community),
    chauvinism in, 15–16, 23–5
    demonstrations, 73–5
    immigration, 59–60, 79–81
    and 1974 war, 98
Loomba, Ania, 14

Makarios (Archbishop Makarios III),
    and EOKA B, 93–4
    EOKA initiations by, 88
    and 1974 war, 95–6, 98, 101–2, 104n1
    and 1960s inter-communal strife, 93
    and Zurich-London agreements, 76–7
Malim, William. *See* Martinengo, Conte Nestore
Mallin, Eric S., 37
Marlowe, Christopher, *The Jew of Malta*, 66
Maronites, 64, 87
Marston, John,
    satirical poems, 32
    The Metamorphosis of Pygmalion's Image, 36
Martinengo, Conte Nestore, *The true report of all the successe of Famagosta*,
    Cypriot demography in, 10–11, 64

Cypriot history in, 66, 78, 88–9, 99
Ottoman conquest of Famagusta and, 29
Massinger, Philip, *The Renegado*, 28
meghali idea, 25, 94, 96
Melas, Pavlos, 93–4, 96
Merchant of Venice, 13, 17, 103–4n4
miscegenation, 18, 40–2, 43, 75
Modon (Methoni), 67, 90–1. See also Egypt: slippage between 'Gypsy' and
Moffett, Thomas, *The silkewormes, and their flies*, 63, 64
Much Ado About Nothing, 36

nationalism (Greek and Turkish), 8, 10–11, 47, 70, 74, 77, 103n1, 107n3. See also EOKA, EOKA B; TMT.
Neill, Michael, 14–15
Newman, Karen, 61
Nicosia
    cabaret industry, 38–9. See also sexuality: during British rule
    Central Prisons, 2, 48–9
    division of, 10, 19, 92
    Famagusta Gate, 21, 87
    Kyrenia Gate, 22
    National Struggle Museums, 21–3, 46, 52–3, 105n4
    Museum of Barbarism, 22–3
    in 1974 war, 95, 98–9
    old town centre, 7, 87–8
    Olympiakos football team, 21, 88
    Ottoman siege of, 13, 97–8
    Pancyprian Gymnasium, 21, 87. See also Durrell, Lawrence.
    Paphos Gate, 87
    Terra Santa school, 87. See also Catholics
    torture cells at Omorphita, 49–50
    start of British rule in, 45
    1974 atrocities, 97–8. See also ethnic cleansing
    1974 and property, 18-23. See also *Apostolides v. Orams*.
    in relation to *Othello*, 23–8

Othello's Tower, 7, 8, 29
Ottomans. See conversion; Cyprus Wars
Ovid, *The Metamorphoses*, Venus in, 30, 32, 35, 41
    Cypriot prostitution and sacrifice in, 30, 32

Palmer, Sir Richard, 38
Papadakis, Yiannis, 20, 40, 105n4
Paphos, 7
    anti-coup radio station. See Free Paphos Radio
    Bishop Gennadios of, 95
    and Pygmalion myth See Marston, John; Pygmalion
    Tree of Handkerchiefs, 69
    in *Venus and Adonis*, 35
Pilla, Eleni, 15, 75

Pory, John. *See* Africanus, Leo
Pygmalion (myth), 36, 38
Pyla detention centre, 49

race. *See* blackness; miscegenation
Richard I, 45, 76. *See also* Crusaders
Rizokarpaso. *See* Dipkarpaz
Ronk, Martha, 33
Rymer, Thomas, 60

St James the Moor Slayer, 12, 78
Seferis, George,
    Logbook III or *Cyprus, Where It Was Ordained For Me*, 75
    and Makarios, 93, 76–7
    'Neophytus the Recluse Speaks', 75–7, 83–4
sexuality,
    in *Othello*'s Cyprus, 32–8, 43–4. *See also* Avity, Pierre d'; Bartholomaeus; Ovid
    during British rule, 38–40
silk production, 59–68
    early modern instructional manuals for, 62–3
    in Cyprus, 59–63, 68–9, 108n1
slavery, 65–6
Smith, Ian, 65
Syria, 67, 87, 99–100

taksim, 107n4, 108–9n1. *See also* TMT
Talat, Mehmet Ali, 52, 69
Titus Andronicus, 35–6
Theobald, Lewis, 36

Thomas, William, *The historie of Italie*, 27–8, 89
'Thunder' (EOKA informant), 79–82. *See also*: EOKA: detention and torture of suspected members of; Nicosia: torture cells at Omorphita
TMT, 53, 92–3, 94, 107n4
torture. *See* EOKA: detention and torture of suspected members of; Nicosia: torture cells at Omorphita; 'Thunder'
Turkish nationalism: *See* nationalism
Türkiyeliler, 83

Varnava, Andrekos, 6, 45, 46, 96, 107n1
Vaughan, Virginia Mason, 8, 78
Venice. *See* Catholics; Cyprus Wars
Venus (goddess),
    as Astarte/Ashtart (Mesopotamian goddess), 40–1, 63
    in British colonial rule, 38–42
    in modern Cyprus, 6
    mosaic by Apelles. *See* Theobald, Lewis.
    in *Othello*, 31–8, 43–4
    and prostituting cults of Cyprus. *See* Avity, Pierre d'; Bartholomaeus; Ovid
    in Shakespeare and early modern literature, 32, 34–7, 67
    and silk, 63–4

Venus and Adonis, 34, 35, 36–7
Vice (medieval allegory), in *Othello*, 44
    in relation to British colonial interrogations, 44–5, 56–7
Vitkus, Daniel J., 14, 65

Walcott, Derek, 'Goats and Monkeys', 75
Winter's Tale, 64
Wells, Stanley, 13
Wolseley, Sir Garnet, 38

Yiorghallas, Makis, 48, 52–3, 88, 102

www.ingramcontent.com/pod-product-compliance
Ingram Content Group UK Ltd.
Pitfield, Milton Keynes, MK11 3LW, UK
UKHW021859220326
469204UK00008B/57

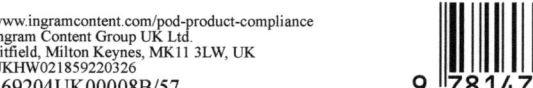